# Talent and Performance

by Eli Ginzberg and John L. Herma

with IVAR E. BERG, CAROL A. BROWN, and

ALICE M. YOHALEM

and JAMES K. ANDERSON and LOIS LIPPER

NEW YORK AND LONDON

 Columbia University Press 1964

to my parents-in-law

Robert and
Zip Szold

# Preface

The best brief description of this study is contained in the 1960 Annual Report of the Carnegie Corporation:

Although we now know a great deal about what happens to the bright youngster in the course of his school career, there has been little systematic study of the careers of talented individuals after they complete their formal schooling. Some gifted young people realize their promise quickly and brilliantly in later life; others do not. A grant to Columbia University will allow Eli Ginzberg to make a study of . . . individuals who were considered highly promising in graduate school ten years ago.

We are indebted to the Carnegie Corporation not only for the generous grant which it made in 1959 for the support of this study, but also for a supplemental grant made in 1962 which permitted the orderly completion of the research. The sympathetic and constructive interest of Dr. John Gardner, President of the Corporation, and Dr. Frederick Jackson, Executive Associate, were a source of added strength for the staff.

As we suggest in chapter 2, the success of this research project depended on the wholehearted collaboration of a large number of officials then at Columbia University. The Vice President, Dr. John A. Krout, initiated the investigation by writing to the fellowship winners we wanted to study and encouraging them to take the time to reply to the lengthy questionnaire that the staff had developed. The late Secretary of the University, Mr. Richard Herpers, and Miss Esther Dudley of his office made it possible for the staff to develop a reliable list of fellowship winners. The Registrar, Mr. Charles Hurd, gave us access to the records of the group and undertook to obtain from other institutions supplemental information which we required.

Mr. Joseph Jefferson and Dr. Mark L. Peisch of the University's Admissions Office enabled us to supplement further our information on the backgrounds of the fellowship group. And we were able to add yet a further dimension through the assistance which we received from Mr. John Bornemann of the University's Placement Office, and Miss Margaret Morgan and Miss Ruth Callan of his staff. The administrative staff at Teachers' College also helped us to develop our list of fellowship winners and provided us with background information about the members of our group who had been on their rolls.

The cooperation of the staff of the University's Central Records Office was crucially important: they gave us a first lead to the present whereabouts of the group we wanted to contact.

This is a relatively small book. But it is based on a large body of information culled from the scholastic records of our group of respondents and from questionnaires they completed. These data and the evaluations based on them were organized into a great many tables which were thoroughly analyzed in the search for significant relationships. Only the most important are presented in the text.

At various stages of the investigation the following

assisted in one or another facet of the processing and interpretation of the material: Erich Goode, Anne Langenberg, Arlene Shafran, William O'Neill, and Stephen Parkoff.

Mr. Parkoff went on to exploit more fully the information which had been gathered about the members of the group who had majored in science or engineering in their undergraduate or graduate studies. He developed a doctoral dissertation based on the fuller analysis of these data. His dissertation, "The Career Development and Utilization of Engineering and Science Graduates," was successfully defended in April, 1964, and copies of it are available in the library of Columbia University.

The following typed successive versions of the manuscript: Gertrude Dacken, Sylvia Leef, Barbara Parkoff, Brenda Richmond, and Virginia Stevens.

Dr. Douglas W. Bray, Director of Personnel Research for American Telephone and Telegraph Company and formerly Research Associate on the Conservation of Human Resources Project, read the book in manuscript and made many suggestions which we incorporated.

Through her skillful editing, Ruth Szold Ginzberg added both to the readability of the text and to the presentation of the statistical materials.

ELI GINZBERG, *Director*
*Conservation of Human Resources*

*Columbia University*
*May, 1964*

# Contents

Preface    vii

1  The Talented and Their Work    1

2  The Participants    11

3  Profile of the Group    26

4  The Shaping of a Career    47

5  Patterns of Career Development    66

6  Measures of Success    89

7  Value Orientations    112

8  Work Satisfactions    137

9  Self-Realization    154

10  Life Styles    177

11  Performance Potential    200

12  The Conservation of Talent    219

Appendix: Questionnaire Used in Career Development Study    239

Bibliography    251

Conservation of Human Resources Project    257

Index    261

# Talent and Performance

# The Talented and Their Work

The word *talent* has many meanings. To some, talent is a quality distinguishable from but closely allied to genius. To others, it encapsulates many of the qualities that are contained within other categories, such as creativity and originality. Some think of talent only in connection with music and the other arts. Others use the term to describe that clear and unmistakable competence or skill that sets an individual off from most of his fellow men, whether it is a skill demonstrated on the baseball diamond, in research, in politics, or in any other arena of life—even in connection with illegal or criminal activities.

In this book we use the term to characterize a group of individuals who have demonstrated a high order of intellectual capability; specifically, each was awarded a fellowship by a major university for graduate or professional study. These talented young people reached the highest rung on the educational ladder short of post-doctoral studies. And at this point they were assessed by those in the best position to judge, their professors, to be outstanding among the students who had reached this level. They were the elite among students pursuing graduate or professional studies within the university orbit. Other students, equally or perhaps even more talented, who were pursuing an advanced course of studies at conservatories, art institutions, or other specialized schools, were excluded from our study by our focus on the university.

The United States and other countries with an advanced technological system need an increasing supply of educated persons to fill the vast and rapidly growing number of professional and technical positions in every sector of the economy—in business, in government, in voluntary organizations, in the professions. Although the experts do not agree that this country has actually been suffering from a shortage of educated persons to fill these posts, few would contest the proposition that every sector of our society could profitably employ additional talented individuals. The authorities also disagree about the available pool of talented persons. The dominant view holds that the proportion of the population capable of pursuing their education to the level of graduate or professional work is severely limited. Social policy can impede or facilitate the efforts of young people to acquire higher education, but even an optimum policy which would eliminate all environmental barriers could move only so far since such a small percent of the population has the intellectual capacity to profit from advanced study.

With our economy demonstrating a continuing strong demand for those with advanced education, and an even stronger demand for those who have demonstrated a high order of competence, the fact that the pool of potential students is limited, possibly severely limited, cannot be lightly brushed aside. Nor has it been. During most of the period since the onset of World War II, and particularly since the launching of Sputnik, leadership groups in the United States have stressed the importance of the conservation of intellectual ability.

Within and outside of government there has been a deep and growing conviction that our security and our welfare depend on our success in this conservation effort. There has been a growing recognition that the true wealth of a country and its basic security depend in the first instance not on its capital plant or its raw materials, nor even on the size of its labor force; they depend on the quality of the leadership in every sector, particularly the intellectual leaders who are responsible for the discovery of new ideas and their translation into economic and social advances.

Most of the new concern with the nurturing of intelligence has been directed to the gifted child and the improvement of the education which he receives. This has been the result of the belief that high intellectual potential is the scarcest and most valuable of all our national resources. It is incumbent on a society which looks ahead to a better tomorrow to take all necessary steps, first, to discover such potential and, second, to cultivate it. In particular, it is argued, a society should remove as many as possible of the obstacles which prevent young people with high potential from acquiring the type of education which will enable them to develop fully their capacities; further, it should take steps to insure that the rewards which attach to certain types of work requiring long training are sufficiently attractive that able young people will be encouraged to prepare for these fields.

As a result of these propositions, which have been widely discussed, efforts have been devoted to increasing the number of able young people who have access to more and improved education. Currently about two-thirds of all young people earn a high school diploma and about half of these graduates enter college. However, relatively little attention has been directed to the experience of these young people after their formal education has been completed. In fact, there have been relatively few studies that have attempted to structure the complexities inherent in the shaping of a career. Some investigators have analyzed the bodies of empirical data available in such compendia as *Who's Who*. In the main this research has sought to classify the background of successful individuals, such as class origins, education, and related facts. These studies have sought to test whether our society today is as open and mobile as in earlier generations. The answer appears to be that this society remains open for those who acquire a good education; for those who do not, advancement is more difficult than in the past.

In recent years, economists and sociologists have analyzed the social antecedents of those who succeeded in reaching the higher levels of business management, for business remains today, as it has long been, the primary arena for work, striving, and success or failure. The studies by Mabel Newcomer and Warner and Abegglen, among others, have revealed that while some of those who arrived at the top levels of American business were the sons of poor men with little formal education, and that many of them did not go beyond high school, this group accounts for a small and constantly diminishing minority. According to these studies, the man with the best prospect of reaching the top or near-top is the one whose father is already well ensconced in business or in a profession and who can provide him with the range of opportunities which will smooth his path.

There are a limited number of related studies of other occupational groups. Some have a focus which is less sociological; their primary aim is to delineate the education, job history, and salary levels of small but strategically important groups of specialists. This has been the aim of the occupational studies carried out by the National Science Foundation.

A different tack was taken by Anne Roe in *The Making of a Scientist*. She identified several groups of scientists and then sought to determine through clinical procedures, such as interviewing in depth and various projective techniques, whether distinctive personality traits characterize scientists in different fields of specialization.

A type of longitudinal approach, both forward and retrospectively oriented, was used by L. M. Terman in his long-range studies of the gifted child. His last report, *The Gifted Group at Mid-Life*, was issued in 1959. Terman and his associates started in 1925 with a careful biometric study of 1,500 gifted young children and, through great ingenuity and perseverance, kept in touch with most of the group and reappraised them from time to time. Terman found that the level of adult performance of the group was distinguished. While some of them had not achieved a substantial measure of success, the vast majority had reached a level of achievement considerably above that attained by those with less intellectual promise.

During the last several years there has also been a burgeoning of interest in "creativity." This has been in part a reflection of our society's need not only for educated men and women, but also for that small minority who have special qualities that enable them to add a new dimension to our life. This interest also reflects the coming of age of dynamic psychology and psychiatry, which encouraged some skillful investigators, such as Donald MacKinnon and Frank Barron at the University of California's Institute of Personality Assessment and Research, to undertake pioneering research into creativity. They are seeking to identify personality characteristics that might help differentiate the highly creative from the merely competent person in such diverse fields as architecture, writing, mathematics, and further to explore whether creative persons in different fields have distinctive personality traits. Their work is significant both for their methods of approaching such a complex subject and for the substantive findings that are beginning to emerge.

These few references, which are limited to work conducted within the United States, indicate that along with the concentration of research on the development of talent, there are at least a few very able investigators who are interested in the dynamics of careers. A listing of all contributions of significant research since the end of World War II alone would include a great many titles. However, with few exceptions most studies of occupational development have not considered the interaction of psychological and sociological determinants. Most of them traveled along one or the other axis. It is the interaction of the two that is at the center of our interest and effort. Perhaps the easiest way to introduce our approach is to cast a backward look at our earlier work.

More than a decade ago we published the results of an exploratory investigation, *Occupational Choice: An Approach to a General Theory* (1951). It had been our intention at the start of that investigation to carry our studies of the individual's development to the point where, having finally crystallized his choice, he confronted the world of work. Would this confrontation lead to an affirmation of his original choice, or would the reality of daily work in his chosen field lead to a reopening and possibly even a complete restructuring of his original choice? We were forced to bring our investigation to a conclusion with a delineation of the process of occupational choice. But during the years since we published the results of our exploration we have looked for an opportunity to follow up our earlier research and carry it forward.

During the intervening years we have pursued our research into the world of work along two major axes. Continuing along the psychological front which provided the framework for our study of occupational choice, we explored related problems such as the handicaps faced by the uneducated, issues in the study of talent, implications of psychiatry for military manpower. Our research culminated in a large-scale investigation of *The Ineffective Soldier: Lessons for Management and the Nation* (1959). We also followed a second tack and explored the institutional aspects of work in a series of studies of the Negro, of young people, and the American worker. In these latter investigations our primary concern was on the way in which changes in the larger society and economy during the past several decades have transformed the role of work in the life of the individual and the nation.

In the present study, we will explore the factors that influence the extent to which people with talent, after completing their education, actually do perform at a high level of competence. For performance is the payoff. The principle of marginality seemed to indicate that since hundreds of investigators are studying the development of talent, it would be worthwhile if a few investigators considered the problem from the vantage point of a realization of potential. We will report on their working lives and experiences, but this is not our sole or even our primary objective. We will then use this information in an attempt to conceptualize a schema which will enable us to perceive more clearly the processes whereby individuals with certain interests, capacities, and values seek to shape careers in a real world with its range of opportunities and barriers. This is an approach to a complicated subject and at best it can succeed only in part. Nevertheless we believe that the attempt should be ventured; at present there is no useful model available which would enable us to study the multiple and sequential decisions which people must make in the shaping of their careers.

At the same time we want to discover the factors that might help to explain why some of our talented group did very well, why others had reasonable success, and why still others faltered along the way. If we can ferret out the relevant factors and learn about their relative importance we will be able to add to the knowledge about the utilization of talent, and then in turn suggest how it could be more effectively conserved.

The conventional way to deal with the results of a research investigation such as this would be to report our findings about the talented group as concisely and objectively as possible and to let it go at that. There might be a speculative chapter at the end to point up questions that were raised that the data could not answer. But convention is not adequate in this instance.

The only way that we could hope to take steps towards the structuring of the process of career development was to follow inductive procedures and to order our material and gross categories with an aim of deriving tentative formulations. More tightly controlled "scientific" studies would have to wait upon the successful completion of this first step.

Very briefly, here are the stepping stones we will establish: The first task is to order the great diversity of career developments into a few distinctive patterns. The next step takes account of the crucial element of achievement as seen by the society that establishes monetary and other rewards for different types of work and different levels of performance. This involves an assessment of the elements of success.

Central to a comprehensive theory of career development is the realization that the individual, especially the talented individual, is constantly confronted with options. What underlies the choices which he makes? Our next step will be to delineate the different value orientations toward work which contain some clues about the factors underlying different behavior with respect to careers.

Whether a person stays within the field for which he has studied and trained or whether he seeks to shift to another depends in the first instance on whether he is able to derive satisfaction from his work. The many and subtle dimensions of work satisfaction are submitted to detailed evaluation. During his preparation for a career in professional, technical, or managerial work the individual must make a series of decisions over a period of at least ten years; almost twice as long must elapse before he becomes established in his career. The crucial importance of time perspective in the process of career development is set out under the rubric of self-realization.

Although decisions about work are of course at the center of the career process, individuals have never devoted all of their time and energy to their jobs, and they are devoting less to this area with every year. An inclusive view of the career process must take into consideration decisions which balance family and other activities against work. We will begin to explore these broader relations.

In the last of the analytical chapters, the focus is on the "performance potential." Here an attempt is made to delineate certain preconditions that help to differentiate the more successful from the less successful individual—preconditions that may be imbedded in his background, his personality, or the societal setting.

These then are the seven basic building blocks for our conceptual framework—career patterns, measures of success, value orientations, work satisfaction, self-realization, life styles, and performance potential. Together they comprise the body of this book.

We decided to use the accounts of the lives and work of a talented group to develop categories to order and assess their experience. We are interested in the talented group, and we will report what we have learned about them. But we are even more interested in using their experiences to help us design a more comprehensive model for the understanding of career development.

# The Participants

Our decision to study the careers of a group of talented people was easier to make than to implement. There are always major hurdles in the paths of investigators concerned with probing broadly or deeply into social issues. Often, the accessibility of subjects dictates the direction of the research. A high proportion of all social research is carried out on captive audiences—students, patients, prisoners, employees.

All research involves compromises: time, money, manpower are always limited. Moreover, the availability of a sample, its purity, the possibility of establishing valid controls are likely to present problems, whose solution must be compromised before work can proceed. Our first task was to find a group of individuals who met our criterion of high intellectual potential. We finally determined upon a group, each of whom had been awarded a fellowship for graduate or professional study in one of the several departments of a major institution, Columbia University. The criterion of selection for these fellowships was academic achievement, not financial need or even an admixture of the two.

When we made this decision we knew that all departments or schools did not have applicants of exactly the same strength, or that the procedures which they followed in assessing the applicants for fellowships were identical. In addition, we recognized the possibility that some applicants who lost out in the competition for a fellowship may have been equal or even superior to those who did receive an award. But those who were awarded fellowships were surely among the ablest students. Our focus was on the process of career development, not on the objectivity of the fellow-ship award procedures. We considered the award of a fellowship as presumptive evidence of superior intellectual performance.

We knew that in limiting our group to individuals who attended graduate or professional school we were restricting our study to a certain range of superior performance. Advanced education is a mandatory or preferred preparation for a large number of careers, but by no means all. In addition to the classic professions of medicine, law, and the-ology, graduate or professional study is the basic route into science, research, and teaching at institutions of higher edu-cation. Moreover, an increasing number of able people who enter engineering, business, journalism, government service have attended graduate or professional schools. Our selec-tion caught a large number. We did not need to catch them all.

We recognized that high potential demonstrated during the preparatory process and later work performance are not always sharply distinguishable. A man's career is not in-dependent of his earlier performance in school. How well a student performs in school, especially as he moves towards the higher grades, is an important determinant of whether he will continue to study. Moreover, his scholastic accom-plishment, especially in graduate school, will have a direct influence on his job prospects. For instance, the editor of the law review is likely to receive many attractive offers of jobs when he graduates. The same preferment is likely to be shown others who have been singled out for special distinction towards the end of their educational preparation.

Nowhere is this nexus between education and career closer than for those who hope to pursue an academic career after completing their doctorate. Their professors are directly involved in helping to fill a wide range of teaching and research positions, from a few that are very attractive to a larger number with limited horizons. At a minimum, a man's record in graduate school will exercise an important influence on the early stages of his career. The halo effect may be pronounced. A young man who has been characterized by his professors as very bright will often have several years of grace before people take a second harder look at him and his work. By the time they do, he may be, and often is, firmly ensconced in an important position from which he cannot be easily dislodged, whatever his actual performance has been.

There is an inevitable relationship between potential and performance. One cannot be treated as independent of the other. Nevertheless, we wanted to delineate as clearly as possible the formative years of a man's career and to evaluate the factors, both personal and those within the larger environment, which help to determine the shape and direction of his career. We therefore decided to concentrate on the first ten to fifteen years of a man's working life.

To study only a restricted period would enable us to sort out and appraise the many relevant factors and their interaction. While we realized that the final shape of a man's career and particularly the level of his achievement might be substantially affected by events of later years, we were impressed with the strategic importance of the period during which he establishes himself. In a great many instances this might determine his later working life.

There was a further reason to restrict the time span of our study. There has been no recent period during which the economic life of the nation was not characterized by both prosperity and depression. It appeared desirable to avoid the major depression of the 1930s with its serious occupational distortions. These were years when even talented university graduates were fortunate if they could acquire a substitute's license to teach high school, and when many young physicians supported themselves by working as temporary clerks in a post office or store.

Any criterion that is used in social research has a limitation as well as an advantage. The desirability of studying career development in a relatively stable economic environment together with our interest in the formative period of a man's career set the time span for the investigation. We decided to restrict our study to those who had been awarded graduate fellowships at Columbia University during the period 1944–45 to 1950–51, a span of six academic years. We decided upon this period even though young men who were completing their advanced studies in the middle and late 1940s had been young children during the depression. These were tumultuous years, and even if contemporary psychology is only partly right about the importance of childhood experiences for adult behavior our sample might have a subtle bias. We could only be alerted to it.

The selection of Columbia was a decision of convenience in many ways. We could readily obtain the names of several hundred individuals whom we hoped to study intensively. Since ours was an exploratory study of career development, not a controlled study of fellowship awards, we did not need to include other institutions in our sample. But above all, we looked forward to receiving the full cooperation of the university authorities in making contact with the former fellowship holders and in enabling us to abstract basic information about their background from university records.

We recognized that restricting our study to Columbia students would probably lead to the inclusion of a relatively large number of New Yorkers, many of foreign extraction or even of foreign birth, and to an overrepresentation of those who attended graduate faculties rather than professional schools. But these appeared to be subtleties that did not outweigh the many clear advantages of using a Columbia group.

After we had developed a roster of names, addresses, and background information of the group who had been awarded fellowships during these six years, we had to find a way of eliciting their cooperation. We had developed and pre-tested a ten-page questionnaire, and had learned that our questionnaire required between two to four hours to answer.

The Vice President of Columbia University at the time, Dr. John A. Krout, who exercised administrative responsibility over the Conservation of Human Resources Project, agreed to send out a letter outlining the study and requesting cooperation in answering the questionnaire. We believe that the good response, both quantitively and qualitatively, reflected in large measure the respect of the recipients for the university and for Dr. Krout. The letter he sent follows:

January 3, 1961

Dear Mr. _____:

I am writing to request your cooperation in connection with a research inquiry that Columbia recently initiated.

The Carnegie Corporation made a grant to the Conservation of Human Resources Project at Columbia to explore the major factors that influence a person's career and performance. Primary attention is being focused on the relationships between a person's advanced education and his later work experience.

These relationships will be explored by studying a sample of men and women who pursued graduate or professional studies at Columbia between 1944 and 1950. You are included in the sample.

Since the only way to secure the basic materials required for such a career study is through the collection of original data, a comprehensive questionnaire has been devised. It is enclosed herewith and we hope you will answer it frankly and fully.

I can assure you that your answers will be treated confidentially and will be evaluated only as part of the analysis of the entire group.

The University believes that the results of this study can make a significant contribution to educational planning as well as to employment practices. I do hope, therefore, that we will have your cooperation. I want you to know that it will be deeply appreciated.

Cordially yours,

JOHN A. KROUT<br>
Vice President of<br>
the University

A few points are worth noting: reference to the Carnegie Corporation's sponsorship may have acted as a spur to some to reply; the fact that no mention was made that those selected had been fellowship winners may have convinced some who had only moderate occupational success to respond; and firm assurance that answers would be treated confidentially and analyzed without identifying individuals undoubtedly proved encouraging.

A total of 548 fellows had been identified from the files in the Secretary's office. Of this number 90 were eliminated for such reasons as their having returned to their native countries after studying at Columbia; their rejecting the fellowship that had been awarded them; their having received a special fellowship for post-doctoral studies. Nine were deceased or institutionalized. It was impossible to establish contact with another 16. A total group of 433 were reached.

One hundred and sixty-nine responded to Dr. Krout's letter; another 113 responded after receiving a follow-up communication from the Director of the Conservation of Human Resources Project. A total of 282 completed the detailed questionnaire, of which 279 answers were usable. We eliminated 3 respondents who were too ill to be employed full time, but we kept in the group a quadriplegic as well as a professor who had been in psychiatric treatment for ten years. An additional 63 answered a short questionnaire which was designed to elicit responses from those who might reply only to more limited questions. This total of 342 usable replies represented 80 percent of the group to whom we sent a questionnaire—more than we had expected.

We were able to find in published and unpublished sources information about a sufficiently large number of those who did not respond to be able to assure ourselves that they did not differ significantly from the rest of the group in their career pattern, level of occupational achievement, and general occupational profile. A comparison between those who used the short-form and those who completed the detailed questionnaire indicated that the former had achieved a somewhat higher degree of occupational success.

There are relatively few studies in which the subjects consider that they are as expert as, if not more than, those who are in charge of the investigation; and there are few studies in which the subjects have an opportunity to make their criticisms of the study known. The present investigation was unusual in both regards. As in any survey some of those questioned refused to cooperate on the ground that it was none of our business. One particularly adamant lawyer wrote, "I respectfully decline to fill out the questionnaire on Career Development Study. I would allow such an invasion of my privacy only under pain of immediate imprisonment. I hope to die of old age before I ever have to fill out such a questionnaire." A professor of history shared these views: "I can think of no sound reason why a man in a free society should be expected to bare his soul for any purpose, to any group." A research scientist in industry scribbled at the bottom of the letter from Dr. Krout: "I consider this project a waste of time, money, and effort; as well as an indirect invasion of my privacy." A member of the Columbia faculty wrote that he was "torn between doing what I had been asked to do and my various reasons for not wanting to do it." He confessed to "harboring an objection to such questionnaires" but went on to say that such objections must be "exceedingly frustrating to those in the social sciences where researchers depend upon the questions being filled out completely, candidly, and in large numbers."

Frustrating as it was when individuals refused to participate on the ground that the information sought was privileged, we understood and even sympathized with their insistence that privacy is a value worth preserving. In our view, far too little attention has been paid to working out procedures which will enable informed individuals to report what they know about important facets of personal or organizational life under conditions that assure anonymity.

An official, presumably in intelligence work overseas, informed us that his superiors refused to permit him to reply. A Canadian returned the original letter with a marginal note: "I am nonrepresentative of this group."

Others felt that their career patterns had been as one said, "so interrupted and mixed about by the demands of the government that any data on job changes, rates of pay, reasons for leaving jobs . . . would surely be unserviceable for the purpose of your study." A subsequent exchange of letters however prompted many of the critics and the skeptics to reply.

As we have noted, most of the group responded affirmatively. Many appeared to share the attitude expressed by the dean of a law school who wrote to Dr. Krout, "I am so greatly indebted to Columbia University, both in my personal and in my professional life that I will be very happy to answer the questionnaire which you sent . . . I shall do my best to answer the questions frankly and fully." How fully is suggested by the fact that more than half of the respondents availed themselves of the opportunity to write additional comments after completing their questionnaires. Almost all who did wrote at least three or four paragraphs, some wrote much more. Among the subjects most frequently expanded upon in these additional comments were educational or job experiences, reference to personal or family problems, or more general reflections on work and careers.

The questionnaire, which is reproduced in full in the Appendix, was divided into six major sections: the respondent's work experience, his activities off the job, education and training, military or civilian war service, family and marriage, and more general questions about past

and future career development. It had not been our intention originally to rely exclusively on a questionnaire,
but the replies which we received to the one used for pretesting indicated that carefully formulated and articulated
questions, comprising a balanced search for objective information and subjective evaluations, could yield a rich
body of information about the career development of the
respondent. Moreover, it early appeared that we would
probably obtain a better return on our resources if we
directed them to structuring and analyzing the data yielded
by the questionnaires than if we allocated part of them for
interviewing in order to obtain supplemental information.

As we have suggested, the respondents were both critical
and restrained. Many wrote us about their serious questions
concerning the approach, methods, or the validity of the
results. In each instance we replied. One center of criticism
related to the appropriateness of the basic instrument—the
questionnaire. Several respondents asked whether there was
any way of our knowing whether the answers which we
received were honest. Our reply was that we did not elicit
highly private information, though many did volunteer
embarrassing or possibly even damaging details about their
lives. Second, nobody felt compelled to answer every question; several refused to give exact information about their
income. Third, it was unlikely that many people would
wilfully forward false information although it was to be
expected that some might make errors of fact. However,
there were two checks on such errors: information in
different parts of the questionnaire could be reviewed for
consistency; and we would check some of the answers
against records to which we had access.

Some were concerned about our reliance on "retrospective data." One sociologist said that "many of the questions call for retrospective interpretation of 'influences' that is inevitably unreliable." Several others argued that this was not a valid way to proceed since only current observation and recording of the reasons why men accept or reject a particular occupational opportunity would reveal the "true" basis for their action. In our replies to these criticisms, we suggested that the passage of time frequently helps the individual to perceive more clearly the forces which underlay a previous action; that the recall of a highly intelligent and young group concerning their occupational development would be good; and, again, that we could check many of the recollections by recourse to existing records.

A distinguished professor of statistics remarked at the end of his questionnaire that "few people are going to answer such searching questions with candor even if they could." And another, an able research chemist, said, "I don't believe that this study probes at all into the psychoanalytic determinants of career development." Several others indicated their concern about a methodology that did not make use of depth psychological techniques. In their opinion, the "true" forces determining the actions and decisions of men are embedded deep in the unconscious and, short of a depth psychological approach, nothing of significance could be learned about them.

Certainly the questionnaire approach can be criticized; any method can. However, any practical application of a depth psychological approach, such as an open-ended interview of several hours would also, in all likelihood, leave untapped materials deeply imbedded in the unconscious. There is no way to bring such material to the surface short of a personal psychoanalysis and even in analytic sessions the unconscious forces operating on an individual's career development often remain hidden because they are outside the therapeutic focus. So we reported in *Occupational Choice* after a critical appraisal of fifty completed therapeutic analyses.

Several respondents commented that filling out the questionnaire had been engrossing; others reported that it had been disturbing. Apparently a considerable number who replied fully as well as those who volunteered to amplify any points on which we desired additional information found that the task of answering the questionnaire gave them an opportunity for some "self-analysis." As one remarked, "An attempt has been made to give reasonably full answers above, partly also in the interests of self-analysis." Another concluded that "this confessional has clarified for me one of my perplexing personal problems but has not yet supplied the answer."

A more important point should be made in this connection. While knowledge of unconscious factors would add to the understanding of the career development of a particular individual, our objective was to develop a conceptual structure for studying a larger group. What one needs to learn about a group of people is often quite different from what is needed to understand a particular individual. Finally, the fact that we were able to order the information about the careers of 342 individuals into a limited number of discrete categories suggests that the propelling factors in their lives might be revealed through their actions, as well as through their words, and sometimes even better.

The replies indicated that a considerable number of respondents, believing that luck, happenstance, or chance held the key to their career development, thought that the questionnaire underplayed the role of social and other environmental factors. Actually, however, the questionnaire provided ample opportunity for discussion of these external factors. Moreover, even the most powerful external factor, such as compulsory military service, does not deprive an individual of all options. Even in a major war, an educated individual has considerable discretion as to the time he enters service, the service he elects to join, whether to become an officer or not, and whether, at the end of hostilities, to maintain an active relationship to the reserves or to cut his ties to the service at the first possible moment.

Although several respondents saw their career development solely in terms of a response to external forces, not every such self-diagnosis was correct. To say, as did one development engineer, "I have never laid plans for the future as have many individuals. Nearly all of my 'breaks' came unexpectedly and with little notice," indicates a particular psychological attitude toward his occupational development rather than a valid analysis.

The final area of skepticism related to more purely methodological considerations. One respondent believed that those who replied early would do so with more "fullness and frankness" than the stragglers. Another questioned whether the replies could be meaningfully summarized. He wrote, "From the viewpoint of a physical scientist a more objective (check-the-appropriate-box) type of questionnaire would have been preferable. . . . How (in an objective way) can you process the data and come to any statistically valid conclusions when you allow such latitude in the type of response to a given question?"

An advertising executive was disturbed about the same point though he did not foreclose the possibility of a successful resolution. He asked, "After several years in Re-search, I must inquire as to how you plan to handle and tabulate all these data? Never saw so many open-ends." Others said that nothing short of their writing a novel or a complete autobiography would provide us with honest answers to the questions.

Most of those who disapproved of our methodology would have preferred an experimental design which would test under rigid conditions the behavior of a few carefully controlled factors. But we were engaged in an exploratory investigation of the interaction of many complex psychological and social factors as the individual makes multiple decisions about his career. We did, in fact, seek to limit the gross variables. The questionnaires yielded several hundred thousand pieces of discrete data which had to be organized before we could proceed to analyze them. We developed a large number of tables each concerned with a different aspect of career development. Since ours was an exploratory study, the data were used not to test the validity of the formulations and generalizations, but rather to serve as a frame for developing them and pointing directions where interpretations might be found.

But even within this limited context we found it desirable to submit them to tests of significance in order to avoid theorizing about differences due to chance. We used the *chi square* test and rejected the null hypothesis for differences at the .05 level. Following a lead of Professor Samuel Stouffer, we relied primarily on "the pattern of the percentages, not on the actual amounts."

We limited the group to individuals who, according to a reasonable operational definition, were highly endowed intellectually; who had pursued their education at least to graduate school; who lived in the United States or Canada. The period under investigation was characterized by good employment opportunities. Finally, the study was restricted to men.

This last point warrants elaboration. We had originally included women fellowship winners. An early examination of their replies indicated, however, that many found the questionnaire unsuitable for reporting the patterning of their lives. Their occupational development was much less clearly structured than that of the men. While the patterning of some women's careers was found to be not significantly different from that of many male respondents, the majority were quite different. In a great many cases the occupational development of the women was a derivative of their predominant life pattern in which husband and children took precedence. We therefore early decided to limit this study to men and to undertake a separate investigation into *The Life Styles of Educated Women*.

# 3

# Profile of the Group

We will introduce the men whose career development forms the center of our investigation with a short summary of their current occupational and family status and their educational background and war service. We will also review here some of the characteristics of the families into which they were born and the circumstances under which they were brought up. Since all of the questionnaires were sent out and returned during the calendar year 1961, the term "present" or "current" refers to the status of the respondents in that year.

Most of the respondents (83 percent) were between 34 and 44 years of age in 1961; 11 percent were between 45 and 51; and the remaining 6 percent were either below 34 or above 51. Their modal age was 40 and an average of fourteen years had passed since they had studied at Columbia. During these years they had started their careers, to raise families, and to fit themselves into the communities in which they had settled.

Since many men confront new challenges in middle and later life and respond to them successfully, we cannot know what will happen to the members of our group as the years go on. However, many reported that they were well established and did not expect any major changes in the general pattern of their lives. Others indicated that they were still striving to find a better occupational adjustment or to improve their position. It is inevitable that even among those who reported that they were "settled," some will meet exigencies which will disturb their present pattern.

All 342 were in the two highest rungs of the occupational ladder: they were either in professional or technical work or they held managerial positions. There was not one exception. The records disclosed that quite a few had worked in lower level jobs after the completion of their education, but these jobs had been interim rather than permanent. In view of their superior endowment and excellent education, their high occupational status is not surprising. But it is remarkable that not a single person was found below the top of the occupational ladder.

The group was roughly divided among the following broad occupational *fields:* one-quarter were in each of the following—humanities, social sciences, physical sciences; the last quarter were in the independent professions such as law, dentistry, engineering, architecture, or in business, either as entrepreneurs or as corporation executives.

In terms of the *functions* which they performed, about half were engaged in teaching or in teaching and research combined. With very few exceptions they were teaching at the collegiate, professional, or graduate level. The other half were distributed almost equally among research or research combined with administration in other than a university setting, general managerial or administrative work, independent professional work, or as professionals working in a staff capacity.

A third way of describing their occupational status is the *institutional setting* within which they worked. Slightly more than half were on the staff of a college, university, or professional school. The next largest group worked for corporate enterprise, and the rest were employed by non-profit organizations or government or were self-employed.

This brief review of the fields, functions, and the institutional settings indicates that the group was very heavily represented in academic and research work. Nor is this surprising: many who pursue graduate or professional education have these specific career objectives in mind.

Since so many were employed by academic institutions, we might expect that their salaries would be relatively low. In point of fact, the figures that were reported did have a downward bias for despite our pretesting, we had failed to ask clearly for total income. One professor pointed this out: "You do not ask for other regular sources of income and amounts and whether these stem from the fact of the primary career. I get regularly $3,000 from two permanent consultantships, and I earn another $2,000 to $3,000 from royalties, lecture fees, consulting, and writing. Thus about 25 percent of my gross income is from outside of the university, yet a consequence of the job. . . . I can earn, therefore, upwards of $25,000 as a professor, and many I know earn more than this." It should be added parenthetically that this respondent was a member of one of the leading academic institutions in the country.

The possibility of other sources of income was called to our attention by an assistant professor of classics who reported an *earned* income of $6,500 per year. "The possession of a small independent income . . . was of decisive importance in permitting me . . . to continue teaching at a salary of $6,500 which by itself does not provide adequate income for raising a family in a satisfactory way in a big

city. If I did not have this modest outside income, I would
be obliged to teach summer school each year and/or to
accept outside work regardless of its intrinsic value, simply
for extra income . . . and this prejudices what seems to
me an absolutely essential part of first-rate university teaching: continuous participation in creative research."

In instances where wives worked, and as will be noted
later these were very limited, total family income was
probably underreported. But this was a minor distortion.

The distribution of reported income which does contain
these downward biases showed that about half the group
earned between $7,500 and $12,500 and another 30 percent
earned between $12,500 and $20,000. The remaining 20
percent were almost equally distributed between those
with incomes below $7,500 and those with incomes above
$20,000.

Four of the respondents are engaged in religious, missionary, or related types of work where they receive no salary
or only a very modest one. One reported; "I am a priest
and a member of a Catholic religious order . . . nor do I
earn a salary. My expenses are paid and all necessities taken
care of by the college and the order."

When allowance is made for the facts that such a high
proportion of the entire group was employed in a sector of
the economy where salary levels are relatively low, that a
few received little or no income, that the earnings which
many reported undoubtedly understated their total family
income, and that the group was still some distance from
achieving its maximum earnings, the finding that only
2 out of 5 earned more than $12,500 is no longer surprising.

Reports of marital status showed that the great majority
(84 percent) are married. Six percent had been married

but are now separated, divorced, or widowed. The remaining 10 percent are still single. About 60 percent of those who are or had been married have either two or three children. The remaining married men are almost equally divided among those who have no children, those who have one child and those who have more than four. There is no unique characteristic of the marital and family patterning of the group.

A quite different finding emerges from a review of their educational background: 72 percent had already earned their doctorates. Since 26 percent of the group were engaged in the practice of the law, journalism, or in other professions where the acquisition of a doctorate is exceptional, and many of the remainder were employed in business or government in an administrative or managerial capacity where a doctorate is not a prerequisite for appointment or promotion, the fact that 7 out of 10 had earned a doctorate is indeed exceptional. In time this ratio will probably increase slightly as a few more men acquire a doctorate.

Of the 245 respondents with doctorates, 3 out of 4 received their degrees not less than six and not more than thirteen years ago. The remaining group is equally divided between those who acquired a degree recently and those who acquired it more than thirteen years ago. It is generally agreed that within six years an individual is likely to derive most of the specific occupational benefits from a doctorate, such as access to jobs which require a degree.

With regard to undergraduate preparation, the largest subgroup, 43 percent, attended Ivy League colleges or small private colleges with high academic standing. About half of this subgroup had attended Columbia College. Another 10 percent were graduates of one of New York

City's public colleges. Almost every other type of institution was represented, small and large, private and public, liberal arts and technical, secular and religious.

Some indication of how different members of the group assessed the influence of their undergraduate training on their careers is suggested by the following excerpts. Among the many who mentioned the stimulation which college had provided was a professor of chemistry at one of the nation's leading universities who wrote that a significant aid to his career development was "attending a small high quality liberal arts college (Grinnell College) in Iowa, which was an accident of my parents' location at the time I was college age. I still feel that this is the best possible preparation for a person going on to graduate school." A director of foreign exchange programs stated that "the broad humanistic training at Columbia College made me socially and intellectually acceptable at Oxford." On the other hand, a professor of history noted that his "undergraduate preparation (at Columbia) was not 'professional,' too general, not demanding enough."

Others who were less positive about the advantage of a liberal arts training included the feature writer of a large metropolitan newspaper. He said, "The school I attended (an Ivy League College) apparently considered its duties discharged upon the completion of my studies. I was cut adrift to fend for myself in a world which is not particularly kind to those who possess a so-called 'liberal arts' education. As a broad intellectual base this education was fine. But for the pursuance of a definite career, and as an aid in earning my own living, this 'training' was practically useless. And to a certain extent my college education was something of a hindrance, since it laid emphasis on the fact that 'man does not live by bread alone.' Unfortunately, I discovered late the importance of 'bread' also—and found that for six years my college and graduate education had been protecting and sheltering me from the necessities of bread winning." Another, a professor of Latin and English in a Southern institution, was sure that "the fact that I could only attend a very small college was a lifelong hardship."

An occasional person went back and singled out his high school education as a major career influence. A senior research scientist wrote, "Good fortune to elect to go to a scientific high school (Stuyvesant High, N.Y.C.) instead of going along with the crowd to get a 'general' high school education. This was a crucial turning point." Yet, a professor of French claimed that he "could have benefited a good deal from a better public school education than the one I received in the New York public schools. Looking back, much of my time during those years was wasted, and I formed a number of bad intellectual habits from which I have not completely freed myself even today." However, most considered their high school experience relatively insignificant. They considered their years at college much more important. Some felt distinctly handicapped by having had to attend (probably because of lack of funds) institutions which had a weak faculty or an uneven curriculum. And some who had attended good colleges questioned whether they had received a sound education. Nevertheless, from the evidence available to us it appears that about 3 out of 4 in the group were satisfied with their college education.

Between 25 and 35 percent of the entire group had attended public institutions where they paid no tuition or where the tuition and fees were very small. The others paid tuition which ranged from $300 to $400 per annum. Room and board were at a commensurate level. With a little support from their families and from scholarships—which many of them had—and with a willingness to earn money during vacations and on weekends, most of the men seemed to have been able to make ends meet without too great difficulty. Some few completed college after their military service which meant that they had GI benefits to help them.

The education of most of the group was interrupted by World War II; others served in the armed forces in the postwar period; and a few were called at the time of the Korean War. Of the entire group, 62 percent were drafted or enlisted in one of the armed services. About 14 percent served for a year or less; the majority served between two and four years; and the remainder were in uniform for a longer period.

Forty-six percent of all those who served in the armed forces were inducted and separated as enlisted men, most of them with the rank of noncommissioned officer. Thirty-seven percent entered as enlisted personnel but attained officer status. The remaining 17 percent spent their entire military service as officers. Since the service-wide ratio of officer to enlisted personnel is roughly 1 to 10, the fact that more than half of our group attained officer status should be noted. Of course, education was a major factor in officer selection, but not even a doctorate assured one of officer status.

The majority of those who did not serve in uniform participated in some type of civilian activity directly related to the war effort. Only 14 percent of the entire group had no specific military or civilian war assignment. But even this minority was affected by the war. One respondent, currently a student counselor in the New England public school system reported, "I attended Columbia College during the war years. The fact that most of my college friends entered service and I did not was frustrating, even demoralizing to me. As a result the last two years of college for me were almost aimless. I could not do the one thing I wanted and so I tended to drift." However, another result of deferment was noted by a professor of sociology who said, "I was 4F because of bad vision. When I was in grad school, there were few men around. I therefore received more help from the faculty. I entered the labor market just as the war ended and was therefore advantaged as compared with veterans."

As we shall see later, while the war interrupted the education and the lives of most of our group, it was by no means a largely negative influence on their career development. Passing reference has already been made to the valuable GI benefits that helped many continue their education in the postwar period. There were other positive effects that the respondents reported, particularly with respect to affording them the time to clarify their occupational goals.

While we did not request detailed information about their parents' backgrounds and did not attempt to abstract all of the data on the records available to us, we did assemble enough to provide us with a rough sketch of the homes from which they came. The native born, plus those born in Canada, accounted for 85 percent of the total. As we would have expected in view of Columbia's location, there was an overrepresentation of individuals born in the Middle Atlantic states.

About half of the foreign born came to the United States

while they were still young and graduated from high school in this country. For the most part their parents were escapees from Hitler or otherwise dislocated by the outbreak of war. A senior research chemist was sent to the United States in 1939 on a three-month educational tour by his well-to-do father who was a manufacturer of building materials in Central Europe. "The outbreak of World War II, together with other circumstances beyond my control, changed my life completely. Fortunately for myself I had to stay in this country . . . in spite of the fact that I did not speak English and did not have any financial resources left."

A research economist reported, "When I was a junior at Columbia College my father died. Since we had almost no accumulated resources as recent refugees from Nazi Germany, I had to take various types of outside employment. . . . This took up to 40 hours a week."

In general, the families of the native born did not move a great deal while our respondents were growing up. As a result, our respondents attended and graduated from high schools in the regions where they had been born or in neighboring areas. There were, however, exceptions. A geologist and paleontologist wrote that "a nomadic childhood with a road building father tended to discourage group activities and encourage scholastic activities, the lone pursuit of my archeological hobby." A professor of history whose father was a college president reported that he had "lived in Turkey and Bulgaria in youth, traveled in Europe, learned languages. This undoubtedly benefited career in modern European history."

With regard to their home communities, the two largest subgroups, together accounting for almost 80 percent, were

equally divided between those who came from large metropolitan centers and those who came from smaller cities. The
remainder, again almost equally divided, came from small
towns or from rural or farm communities.

As we suggested in the preceding chapter, our selection
of Columbia was likely to lead to a relatively high proportion of students with foreign-born parents, and this was
in fact the case. Almost half the fathers had been born
abroad, the largest number in Eastern Europe, the next
largest in Great Britain and Western Europe. A professor
of French whose parents were born in Turkey said, "not
being Americans by birth, my parents helped to form the
high value that I set from the start on an intellectual career.
Among Armenians, as among most civilized nations, an
intellectual or university professor is regarded with far
greater esteem than by the American public. This undoubtedly had much to do with my early choice of that
particular profession."

With regard to the occupation of the fathers of our
respondents, slightly more than one-fifth were professionals,
and slightly less than this proportion were managers or
businessmen. Thus roughly 2 out of 5 were in the two
highest occupational classifications. About the same proportion, 2 out of 5, were in semiprofessional or clerical
occupations or were small retail proprietors. The remainder
were blue collar workers or farmers.

With regard to the occupations of the mothers, our
questionnaire asked only whether they had worked after
marriage; we therefore do not know whether they worked
before they married. Approximately 2 out of 3 reported
that their mothers had never worked after marriage. The
largest group of working mothers had been employed in

semiprofessional or clerical work; the next largest group had been blue collar workers. A very few had been professionals or had held managerial positions. A number had been the proprietors of small retail establishments.

The families into which the group had been born and brought up influenced to a greater or lesser degree their intellectual development, their educational opportunities, and their career choices. A few quotations will indicate the wide range of conditions and circumstances that characterized their homes. A leading theoretical physicist described his: "A home in which good books were always available and in which a high value was placed on intellectual achievement." An educational consultant whose father was an English professor reported, "Ever since I could remember, my parents' house was a meeting place for intellectuals. There was never a time when I didn't meet academic people, some of whom took an interest in me long before I attended college and graduate school." Another respondent wrote, "The major factor influencing my career in journalism and the related business of public relations in which I am now engaged was my parents' literary interests. My father was a voracious reader who constantly read aloud to the family and evoked an interest in books and writing among his children. My mother, an ex-school teacher, was interested in writing, and although she never created anything important she was forever writing magazine articles, addresses, speeches for other people, letters to the editor. . . . Of my parents' six children five are now engaged in journalism or some allied field."

An assistant professor of foreign languages said that "my family background was extremely important in shaping my interests and later, my choice of career. For example

I was extremely interested in foreign languages as a child largely because my mother and father, particularly the latter, spoke several languages. . . . My father was a typical European intellectual and I admired his ability to speak in different foreign languages with friends."

An oil geologist reported that "father's being a chemistry professor guided me into a scientific field." A professor of history said, "Both parents had their doctorates, both had taught, and the academic career seemed a natural one." A somewhat different result is indicated by the remark of an advertising account executive who said, "My parents allowed me to pursue my own interests freely, did not attempt to direct me toward my father's profession (dentistry) even though it was a logical and sound course that I might have followed." And a dean of a liberal arts college appreciated that he "was fortunate in having had parents in an economic class in which they could send me to a high prestige college."

But the path for others was much more tortuous. An associate professor of philosophy remarked, "I *needed* to do well. My father abandoned us when I was six." A member of the philosophy department of a women's college who had emigrated to the United States from a village in Ireland at the age of 15 indicated that it had been a "long, long and winding road. . . . I had never seen a movie, never talked over the telephone, thought that frost falls from the sky, and believed all women virtuous. I had to learn almost everything the hard way."

A native-born respondent, an economist, whose father had been a dock worker pointed out that the atmosphere in his home hindered his career development, "mainly by limiting horizons and awareness of what income and career possibilities were open to me." Another wrote, "We came from a poor family where outlook was only for factory work. But Mother inspired children to get a college education and seek more satisfying work." The respondent is now a journalist. A research urologist said, "If the lack of encouragement or the inability to offer financial support be considered a negative factor in seeking a career, be that as it may. However, being aware of my family's financial status and lack of interest in higher education . . . I did not expect either encouragement or support and hence felt no lack. My parents did not discourage my efforts in seeking a career but would have preferred that I seek a good paying job for the security which they lacked."

Since the group was growing up at the time when the American economy was racked by a major depression, it is surprising that relatively few commented on this. Some did. "The difficulty that I find in spending money even now traces back to the chronic penury of those years," wrote one. Another reported, "I always felt the perils of poverty and the insecurity of frequent unemployment." Somewhat more frequent were such comments as that the family's "low level of income limited my choice of graduate school."

In some instances, a parent died when our respondent was young; in others, a parent became seriously ill. A chemistry professor noted that the "early death of father when I was 4 years old, and of mother when I was 15 certainly had a profound detrimental effect." While such a situation deprived them of important supports, it did not always have a clearly negative effect on their career development. An assistant professor of classics reported, "Father's early death meant that I had inherited property at age 21 and was to

some extent financially independent as a graduate student."
A senior official of a major industrial organization wrote,
"Parents divorced when I was about 6; no contact with
father afterwards. Mother business-minded, undoubtedly
stimulated interest in business and through it economics
(rather than say, engineering or religion)."

Another, an associate professor of philosophy, realized
that a specific event which would usually be a hardship, the
divorce of his parents, did not have a solely negative influence. "Parents were divorced with consequent social
and economic stresses; on the one hand these factors were
hindrances; but on the other I believe they caused me to
seek the 'escape' of academic life both as a student and in
my career choice." A highly successful chemical manufacturer saw that his "father's illness, limited family income,
and isolated ranch life contributed to diligence in work and
school."

The degree to which the objective environment might
have different subjective implications is suggested by the
music professor who wrote, "My father living in comfortable circumstances up to this year and providing me with
luxurious living accommodations, car, etc., I have not
spurred myself into completing my doctoral dissertation."

The quality of these excerpts, both by what they include
and what they exclude or minimize, together with the data
reported about parental occupations and related information
permits us to summarize the facts about the families in which
the respondents grew up and the influence of their family
circumstances and atmosphere on their career development.

The fathers of between a fifth and a fourth of the entire
group were professional men and presumably had a positive
attitude towards their children's pursuing a higher edu-

cation. There was a sizable additional group of parents who encouraged their children to get as much education as possible and to prepare themselves for professional or technical work. For instance, a professor of microbiology, the son of a tailor, states, "Although on the verge of poverty, parents encouraged education rather than attempting to influence me to drop school and become a wage-earner." Sometimes the mother was the stronger protagonist of education. For example, a book publisher whose widowed mother worked at "whatever she could to keep our family together" said that "my education stemmed from my mother's determination to give me an opportunity to go to college. I think this veneration of learning and respect for books probably carry over to my present situation." We can say then that the home atmosphere of our group was strongly positive with respect to higher education in not less than half and probably considerably more of the families.

There was very little conflict between the generations on the subject of the career choices of our respondents. At least they did not recall or report such conflict. There was one clear exception: "The pressure to join the family business and my prolonged resistance to it by Fabian tactics produced an extended period of uncertainty about my career which caused me to make an unusually late start." Others reported some limited tension. An associate professor of geology at a leading eastern university said that "although I always had strong scientific leanings which my father respected and encouraged, he never really understood how people made a living at it and used to think it was something you did for a hobby outside of a *real* job in the workaday world." An economics professor wrote, "I suspect my father's struggles during the depression reinforced my reluctance to go into business with him."

Additional information about the circumstances of the families from which the respondents came can be derived from their answers about the manner in which they financed their education. The group contained no one with an independent income sufficient to enable him to stretch out his years of study without giving a thought to earning a living. Twice as many (40 percent) reported that their parents' financial circumstances were such as to hinder their pursuing graduate education as reported that these circumstances were a help. With respect to the GI Bill over half specifically mentioned it as a positive factor. Since only 62 percent had seen military service and some of these were entitled to only modest benefits, it would appear that all who were entitled to veterans' benefits took advantage of them.

An associate professor of modern languages remembered that the "GI Bill made it possible for me to become independent of my family when I most needed it. I should hardly have continued if I had to do it on my parents' money." The dean of a graduate school and professor of history also reported that the GI Bill had a determining importance for his career: "The GI Bill and a university fellowship from Columbia made it financially possible to finish my Ph.D. . . . Without that aid I would have left with an M.A. and become a high school teacher."

Many of those without financial assistance from home or substantial veterans' benefits had to go to work, part time or full time, in order to earn enough to continue their graduate studies. About half of the group reported that they had worked while in graduate school, some at considerable cost to their studies.

One of the few respondents who is teaching in a secondary school, but who is the head of his department, reported on his years of graduate study: "Financial resources inadequate so full time night work (8 hours . . . 3 to 11 p.m.) made completion of graduate work impossible." A chief reference librarian said, "I had to spend too much time earning a living to do justice to my course work and desirable supplemental reading as a graduate student." Some found the task of earning a living and earning a doctorate at the same time more than they could cope with and gave up in the middle of their studies to take a full-time job. However, others who worked while in graduate school reported more positive effects: "Need to work thru entire undergraduate and graduate training caused me to buckle down and waste no time and appreciate education."

One additional dimension must be considered. Sixty percent of the students married at some point before they completed their graduate studies. However, marriage was not necessarily an additional financial burden. This depended on whether the wife was able to work or whether she had to care for young children at home.

Of those who were married in graduate school, 44 percent reported that while they were in graduate school their wives had worked most of the time and another 23 percent stated that their wives had worked some of the time. Thus 2 out of 3 of the married group were assisted while in graduate school by wives who worked. Many conveyed, if less poetically, sentiments such as these: "The loyal, self-sacrificing help of my wife has been by far the most important factor in my career development." "My wife 'worked my way' through Columbia's graduate school." Another states, "My wife had a small income which, with her interest in my return to school was an essential factor in my ability to do it." One man reported that his in-laws were sufficiently affluent that they were able and willing to defray his living expenses and tuition while in graduate school. Others who married before the completion of their graduate studies, particularly those who had children, mentioned the financial burden created by a family. A professor of history wrote, "It is possible that the responsibilities of marriage and parenthood immediately after the war, may have slowed down my completing Ph.D."

Finally, the respondents were aided in financing their graduate education through fellowship awards. For the year during which they held the Columbia fellowship most of all of their expenses were covered. During the course of their graduate studies about half of the group held one or more additional fellowships, scholarships, or grants in aid. One-third held at least one additional fellowship.

Despite the substantial economic pressure on so many of these young men, apparently no one thought of borrowing money in order to finish his studies more expeditiously. At least no one made any reference to loans. This was an approach that had not yet become institutionalized.

From the data available to us we cannot make even a rough distribution of the income of the respondents' parents at the time the respondents were nearing the end of their formal education. But a few generalizations can be ventured: only a handful indicated that their parents met their full expenses in graduate school. Many could and did in fact make a partial contribution. Others could make none. The largest group of families were "lower middle class."

To round out what we know about the major characteristics of the group, we might add that only two were Negroes and four were Chinese.

We had sufficient information to classify 70 percent of the group according to their religious affiliation. Roughly half were Protestants, a third were Jewish, and the remainder were Catholics. The relatively high proportion of Jews reflects in considerable measure the location of Columbia University in New York City and the intellectual and occupational orientation of urban Jews; the relatively low proportion of Catholics is consistent with the findings of other investigations that in general Catholics are underrepresented among those pursuing higher education.

Two brief summaries of the group can be ventured. The first is descriptive, the second interpretive. First, the respondents were predominantly a second generation native-born urban group, drawn from all parts of the United States, but heavily from the Middle Atlantic states. Their parents were in modest economic circumstances and had higher educational and cultural achievement and aspirations than their occupational standing. The largest group were Protestants. They had attended good colleges and most of them had served in the Armed Forces. The majority married during graduate school. A very high proportion had secured a doctorate, and all were earning their livelihood in professional or managerial work.

The interpretive summary, which is also more speculative, includes the following: these individuals had parents in modest circumstances but most of them encouraged their children to strive for a higher place in American society. Strongly endowed intellectually, the respondents did well in school. They did well in the Armed Services. They had enough inner direction so that the war did not deflect them from their chosen occupational goals; most of them continued their education until they had acquired a doctorate. Ten to fifteen years after graduate school finds them married, with a conventional number of children, fitting into the communities into which they had settled. They were holding down responsible positions in academic life, business, and government. Almost without exception they were making good use of their education and training.

# 4

## The Shaping of a Career

The three major strands that individually and collectively help to shape an individual's career are educational preparation, occupational choice, and early work experience. These in turn are likely to be affected by two other major life experiences—military service, particularly during the course of a war, and marriage and children. Military service is a specific interruption to education or work plans; marriage and children introduce important new considerations that must be weighed in relation to career objectives.

Running through these strands and conditions is the central element of time: a man can reach an occupational decision early or late; he can proceed straight through school, or he can interrupt his studies, one or more times, to go to work. In fact, as he nears the end of his educational preparation he may decide to do both in tandem—study and work. The question of whether he marries early or late and, even more important, whether there are children early or late will affect his margins of freedom with respect to his career choices. During the last quarter century the age at which a young man entered the Armed Forces and the length of time he served were likely to exercise an important influence on his career plans and later actions.

The following analysis will set out what we know about

each of these facets in order to gain a first insight into the manner in which the respondents' careers took shape.

As we pointed out in *Occupational Choice,* many young people complete their formal schooling before they have matured sufficiently, either intellectually or emotionally, to be able to crystallize their decision about an occupation. But this did not apply to the present group whose education did not terminate with the tenth or twelfth grade, when they were 16 or 18, but usually continued until they had acquired a doctorate after almost 20 years in school. Few persons can afford, or desire, to continue to study for study's sake beyond their baccalaureate, and our group was no exception. As we noted earlier, the linkage between educational preparation and occupational achievement was particularly close for most of the group. The successful completion of higher education is the only, or surely the preferred, access to the professions. And the many who looked forward to an academic career in teaching or research or a combination of both also required a doctorate if they hoped to advance.

The willingness of individuals to pursue their education for such long periods and to undertake the costs, including that of foregoing income they could have had from a job, must be deeply rooted in their career plans. They must very much want to pursue a particular career. Of course, they may enjoy studying; some may even continue to study because they enjoy it or because they are afraid to start to work in what appears to be a very cold world. But on balance we must postulate that it was their career plans that provided the direction for the ways in which this group met and resolved the options that they faced along the way. Therefore we will begin our more detailed analysis by setting forth what we know about the occupational choices of the respondents.

In our study of *Occupational Choice* we pointed out that
even very young children speculate about what they want
to be when they grow up. However, the child's ideas of his
role as an adult are rooted in fantasy and take no account
of the reality of the nature of the work or of the necessity
to qualify for any particular occupation. The child responds to selective aspects of the work of adults largely
through identification with key persons, particularly his
parents.

The passage of years and the child's exposure to school
and his responses to it result in a slow but steady replace-
ment of the fantasy base by reality considerations. Through
the courses which he likes and those which he finds un-
interesting or boring and which he comes to reject, the
young person begins to learn a little about his interests.
From the marks which he gets he learns a little more about
his capacities, both his strengths and weaknesses. By the
excitement he experiences as well as by the enthusiasms his
teachers, peers, and others evoke in him, he becomes more
aware of his emerging values and goals. By adolescence,
he is able to introduce into the occupational equation the
reality considerations involved in preparing for different
types of careers and the opportunities and limitations in
pursuing one or another. At this time a young person from
a modest family who had thought of becoming a physician comes to realize the costs in dollars and time involved
in preparing for a medical career.

These tentative probings and attempts to clarify one's
occupational goals continue until they begin to provide a
solid base on which concrete career decisions can be built.
A basic question relates to the time at which this solidifi-
cation of interests takes place. According to our earlier study
a significant proportion of young people in college appear

to crystallize their occupational choices during their junior year, that is, as they approach the end of their teens. Of course some reach this stage of crystallization earlier and others considerably later. In the present investigation, which was primarily concerned with the experiences of talented people after they had completed their education and had begun to work, we collected only a minimum of information about their occupational choice determination. But that minimum provided us with an opportunity to check out our earlier findings and to note the connections between early career plans, educational preparation, and work experience of the members of our group.

An important finding which has bearing on the stabilization of their occupational choices was that 60 percent of our group pursued as their major subject in graduate school the subject which they had selected as their undergraduate major. Another 30 percent selected a major in graduate school that was related to their major in college. Only 10 percent made a radical shift after college.

Table 1 presents a distribution of our group in undergraduate and graduate school by the major subject studied.

A casual inspection reveals a high order of congruence between the fields selected by the group in undergraduate and in graduate school. The declines in English and history must be read against the gains in "other professional fields," which include journalism and law for which English and history are conventional preparation. The fit is close particularly since those who followed "two fields" concentrated in the same or closely allied disciplines.

Another indication of stabilization of interest, at least with regard to major field of study, is the relation between the respondent's major in graduate school and his field of

TABLE 1. *Fields of study in undergraduate and graduate school, in percent*

| Field | Undergraduate (N = 278)* | Graduate (N = 342) |
|---|---|---|
| English | 11 | 8 |
| Other humanities | 11 | 13 |
| History | 11 | 9 |
| Other social sciences | 17 | 14 |
| Chemistry | 15 | 11 |
| Other natural sciences | 11 | 11 |
| Engineering | 11 | 10 |
| Other professional fields | 9 | 16 |
| Two fields | 4 | 8 |
| Total | 100 | 100 |

* No information available for 64 respondents.

work. Until he confronts the reality of work no individual can know whether his plans, indeed his choice, were sound or not. In the four major fields of work within which such a test could be made—humanities (including journalism and education), social sciences, natural sciences, and engineering—we found that 5 out of 6 respondents maintained their interest as indicated by their major in graduate school in their field of work. Since these occupational categories are gross, the parallel between majors in graduate school and later work must be interpreted loosely. Nevertheless, the congruence can be taken as further evidence of marked stability.

Answers to the questionnaire enabled us to estimate the approximate age at which the respondents crystallized their occupational goals. Just under three-quarters of the entire group (72 percent) reported that their occupational goal was related to their later actual field of work first in college;

22 percent said that this happened in graduate school; only 6 percent stated that they completed their formal education without having crystallized an occupational goal that was related to their later work. That college was the period during which most of the respondents reached a choice about their future work is underscored by the additional finding that only about one-third of the group had an occupational goal in college that was unconnected with their later work.

In hoping to explore a little further the informative factors related to occupational choice and career development, we had included the following question: "As you look over your working life, can you identify any persons who played a key role in your career, particularly with respect to influencing the nature and character of your work?" While more than 3 out of 4 (78 percent) singled out an individual who had exercised a dominant influence on their development, the influence of these key persons for the most part was related less to the respondents' occupational choice than to their work adjustment. Only 1 in about 7 indicated that he had been strongly influenced by some individual in his choice of a field, but almost half reported that the particular specialty that they had entered or the particular employment situation in which they found themselves was the result of the influence of a key person.

Teachers, at every level from high school to graduate school, were most frequently singled out as having played an important role; the only other group of individuals mentioned with any frequency were employers. Only a very few referred to relatives. Among those who indicated that their occupational choice or later career development had been directly influenced by a key person was a professor of chemistry who reported that "a high school chemistry teacher developed my interest and gave me a strong background." Another chemistry professor said, "A fellow student at Columbia College convinced me that I should be a chemist rather than a chemical engineer. Also, my thesis preceptor convinced me that I should be a university professor rather than an industrial chemist."

A social science analyst wrote that "a very inspiring professor in an introductory course . . . stimulated my interest in the field I subsequently chose as my life work." Another respondent mentioned a deceased professor at his college who "literally pulled me out of the doldrums after service and kept me on the goal of admittance to Columbia Graduate School of Journalism." And a computer researcher cited "physicist friends who suggested computers as good applied math field." These brief excerpts provide a little indication of the multitudinous ways in which key persons affected the careers of various members of the group.

These data supplement some earlier data about the manner in which the respondents moved towards the crystallization of occupational choice and the specification of work goals. We saw in the preceding chapter that parents often influenced their values with respect to higher education and professional or scientific work. In this chapter we note the influence of the educational process. Young people must make choices in college and in graduate school with respect to a major subject and these choices usually bring them closer to a clarification of their occupational goals. In the present group the majority had fairly well determined these goals before they had completed their undergraduate studies. In the process of clarifying these goals their teachers played a key role, less with respect to their basic occupational choice than in their later actual employment situation or their adjustment to it.

As we suggested earlier, the steady progress of the individual through the school system becomes less ordered as he nears the end of his undergraduate education. For then he confronts a large number of conflicting and complicating pressures and pulls: military service, graduate education, marriage, work. The way he makes his choices at this time will significantly influence the initial shaping of his career. Sometimes these pressures begin to operate even before he has completed college. Table 2 presents the ages at which the men in our group completed their undergraduate studies.

TABLE 2. *Age at college graduation, in percent* (N = 342)

| Age | Percent | Cumulative Percent |
|---|---|---|
| 18–19 | 4 | 4 |
| 20–21 | 41 | 45 |
| 22–23 | 34 | 79 |
| 24–25 | 12 | 91 |
| 26–27 | 5 | 96 |
| 28 or older | 4 | 100 |
| Total | 100 | |

That a considerable proportion of the entire group graduated relatively late is explained by the fact that of those who had military service—more than 3 out of 5—about half went on active duty before they were 21. And, it will be recalled, they served an average of from two to three years.

Since the doctoral degree plays an important role in determining the career advancement of men who enter academic or research work, the time they spend in acquiring it is an important factor in their occupational development.

Table 3 presents the number of years which elapsed between college graduation and the acquisition of a doctorate.

TABLE 3. *Number of years between baccalaureate and doctorate,
in percent* (N = 245)

| Years | Percent | Cumulative Percent |
|---|---|---|
| 1–2 | 1 | 1 |
| 3–4 | 13 | 14 |
| 5–6 | 19 | 33 |
| 7–8 | 17 | 50 |
| 9–10 | 16 | 66 |
| 11–12 | 11 | 77 |
| 13–14 | 6 | 83 |
| 15–16 | 9 | 92 |
| 17 or more | 8 | 100 |
| Total | 100 | |

It is possible for an able student to acquire his doctorate
in three years after graduating from college, or surely
within four years. Allowing for an average interruption for
military service, it can be said that those who secured their
doctorates within six years after graduating from college
acquired them expeditiously. But only one-third achieved
their advanced degree within this time.

Those who did not serve in the Armed Forces were more
likely to get their doctorate and were more likely to get it
earlier than those whose education was interrupted by a tour
of military duty. Nevertheless, a somewhat higher proportion of those with no military service received their doctorates after a longer period than those who did serve. The
reasons are obscure, but they may be connected with the
fact that the veterans were better able to finance their
graduate education.

One additional finding is relevant: of those who served
at an older age, 17 out of 18 had their doctorate when they

were inducted. Apparently the Armed Services were willing to wait until they had completed their education before requiring that they serve.

For most, military service appeared to be an interruption, little more. Forty percent indicated that it had had "little or no influence" on their career. Only 7 percent stated that it had "delayed" their career development. The others indicated that it had helped to reinforce their original choice, facilitated their continuing with their education, or had aided them to specify the nature of their work.

Much the same picture emerges with respect to the young men who did not serve on active duty but who entered civilian war work or whose careers were otherwise affected by the war. Forty-four percent reported that their civilian wartime activities had had "little or no influence"; 18 percent reported that this experience helped reinforce their original choice; and another 17 percent said that it had helped them to specify their choice.

We inquired of those who had had civilian war-connected work experiences whether in the absence of war they would have entered such work; 32 percent said yes, 58 percent said no, and the remaining 10 percent did not know. Since so many accepted war-connected civilian employment outside their field, it is not surprising that only 1 in 6 indicated that the experience had helped them to specify their occupational choice.

There was one final question bearing on the impact of the war on the career development of the group. We inquired whether the "world situation" had had any influence on their careers. Two-thirds replied that it had "little or no influence." Most of the others indicated that it had had a positive influence with respect to career choice, job opportunity, specialization, or opportunity for further schooling, in that order. Only a very few indicated that it had had a negative effect such as to delay their career development.

The extent of the influence of the war on their career development is suggested by the following. One respondent remarked, "Military service gave me an enforced break, time to think and set a definite goal. GI Bill aided study." Another said, "If I had not been in service for four years, but had gone directly to industry from college I doubt that I would have been stimulated to go on to graduate school. GI Bill was an added stimulating factor." An academician said in retrospect that "my first classroom teaching experience was in the Air Force (1944). It confirmed my growing inclination to pursue graduate work and a career in teaching." Reinforcement of a career choice is demonstrated by the experience of a professor of Japanese whose war service had "an enormous influence. I was given indispensable training in Japanese and strengthened in what was a weak inclination to devote myself to oriental studies."

A professor of philosophy changed his occupational choice after his military service: "Prior to military service I intended to go into engineering, but perhaps the year or so away from school led to a change in orientation. The GI Bill and fellowships were of considerable help." And a market research director who served first as a personnel officer and then as a petroleum officer stated that he had "changed field of academic training from journalism to business administration."

A balance between the positive and negative consequences of service is suggested by the following comments: "Military experience slowed up entrance to graduate school; GI Bill made it possible to complete work faster after war."

The negative influence of military duty was felt by the professor of economics who said, "I believe the war did not affect the choice of my career, but I believe I would have embarked on it three years earlier than I did. On the whole, I judge that the postponement detracted more than it contributed to my progress." However, no one who has had an opportunity to teach veterans can doubt that a considerable part of the time that they "lost" was made up by their greater motivation for study and their greater application to their work.

In view of its scale and the altered conditions that were brought in its wake, it appears that the war had less effect on the career development of our group than might have been anticipated. The war brought changes into the patterning of their lives, but the changes proved to be transitory rather than permanent.

The third important determinant in the shaping of a young man's career is the age at which he marries. The data are presented in Table 4.

As we have noted, 34 had not married. Of those who did, slightly more than one-fourth married at a young age—before their 24th birthday, and only a small proportion married late.

We have noted that a high proportion of the entire group had married while in graduate school, and that in a great number of cases their pursuit of a graduate degree had been assisted by their wives' working, part time or full time. In a period of full employment, such as characterized the post-World War II period, and when the earlier prejudice against employing married women had substantially receded, a graduate student with a wife was in a favorable position to accelerate the completion of his studies and to gain a firm footing in his profession—if the wife were able and willing to work. Aside from economic considerations, many students found much stimulation and added meaning to their lives as

TABLE 4. *Age at first marriage, in percent* (N = 299)*

| Age | Percent | Cumulative Percent |
|---|---|---|
| 18–20 | 2 | 2 |
| 21–23 | 25 | 27 |
| 24–26 | 31 | 58 |
| 27–29 | 26 | 84 |
| 30–32 | 8 | 92 |
| 33–35 | 4 | 96 |
| 35–38 | 3 | 99 |
| 39 or older | 1 | 100 |
| Total | 100 | |

* Age of 9 respondents unknown.

a consequence of their marrying and were able to make a more purposeful use of their time and energies.

While marriage frequently made it easier for many of the young men to speed their graduate education, the birth of children usually turned the scales and made it more difficult, for most of the wives stopped working when they became mothers. Table 5 shows the age of a respondent when his first child was born.

TABLE 5. *Age at birth of first child, in percent* (N = 266)

| Age | Percent | Cumulative Percent |
|---|---|---|
| 21–24 | 8 | 8 |
| 25–28 | 28 | 36 |
| 29–32 | 39 | 75 |
| 33–36 | 16 | 91 |
| 37–40 | 6 | 97 |
| 41 or older | 2 | 99 |
| Not known | 1 | 100 |
| Total | 100 | |

More than one-third of those who had children became fathers before they were 28 and three-quarters before they reached 32. The majority had their first child before they acquired their doctorate. Of the 155 men who had not acquired a doctorate when their first child was born, 77 (or just 50 percent) did not get one. Children proved to be a handicap in this regard. Since only two-thirds of those who had children early—before they were 28—earned a doctorate, in contrast to three-quarters of those whose first child was born after they were 37, it would appear that to some extent the need to support a family did interfere with a man's completing his advanced studies.

At what point in their development did the respondents begin to work full time and how was this connected, if at all, with their other important decisions affecting the acquisition of a doctorate, marriage, start of a family? The first full-time job held by a respondent was not necessarily in the area of his career choice. A considerable number had to go to work relatively early and some had to take whatever job was available. Almost a quarter of the group was at work full time before the age of 23 and two-thirds before their twenty-eighth year. Knowing what we do about the age at which they acquired a doctorate, we can conclude that many began to work regularly before they had completed their studies.

On the basis of information describing about 70 percent of the group, we find that about one-third received a starting salary of under $2,500; about half were paid between $2,500 and $4,500; and most of the remainder received between $4,500 and $5,500. Only 5 percent earned an annual salary of more than $5,500 on their first job. These salaries must be appraised in light of two considerations: many went to work shortly after they had acquired a baccalaureate degree, and they were at work in these first jobs shortly after World War II when wages and salaries had not yet been radically affected by inflationary trends.

As will be recalled, one of the reasons that this group was selected for our investigation was that the period during which they established their careers coincided with a prolonged period of high level employment. Almost 9 out of 10 reported that after they had started to work regularly there were no periods when they had been unemployed. The small minority who reported that they had been without work at some time were evenly divided between those who had been unemployed for less than one year and those who had been out of work for more than a year. Personal circumstances, such as illness, were the most common reasons for their not working. Only a few indicated that they had trouble in finding employment.

The following quotations indicate some of the ways in which the respondents saw the connections among their graduate studies, their marriage, and their first jobs. A librarian: "Work at Rockland State Hospital at nights denied me essential time in library and at my studies and made it impossible for me to prepare for Ph.D. orals and dissertation. Yet I learned much about handling overemotional people." A college teacher: "I probably would have been better off by going directly into teaching in 1947 rather than having gone with T———— Insurance Co. The insurance job was pretty dull and hardly contributed any experience or skill I wouldn't have had anyway."

Others indicated a sense of deprivation because they had had to work before completing their education. "Earlier jobs always meant taking time, precious time from academic work, which made academic competition much more difficult to meet." A professor of history stressed the adverse effects of "lack of money which made work essential" and added that the war "cut such a deep wedge in one's life." In his opinion, "Only for those in public life has war experience been a help."

An assistant professor of English highlights the cross pressures that many who married and had children encountered: "Briefly the Ph.D. struggle, with a full-time job and a growing family, though full of rewards, became a treadmill. Nevertheless, I was about to finish the dissertation when our younger son developed diabetes. The early years of the disease required exacting and constant care on the part of both myself and his mother."

Another assistant professor of history ascribed his slow academic progress to the "need to take a job before completing my planned program of graduate work at Columbia." A professor of music reported that "family and teaching responsibilities after World War II prevented me from devoting sufficient time to my graduate studies." A senior social scientist said that "early marriage coincident with family responsibilities and graduate training were of course significant factors in shaping my early years as a student and a young Ph.D."

But in the comments of a highly successful research manager of a large chemical company we read, "My wife's willingness to work and to subsist happily on the GI Bill and recompense of graduate assistant and fellowships undoubtedly facilitated the completion of my graduate studies." Additional quotations could be presented that would point up that marriage and children spurred some on to achieve their degrees more quickly, while in other instances the additional family responsibilities brought a shift in direction, either temporarily or permanently, as men left their studies to get a job and income.

There were a few additional indications about the way in which the respondents met the multiple challenges of adulthood. First, war service seemed to provide some who were restless with school and uncertain about their future with a forced change of environment which helped to clarify their goals. Second, although our group should have been informed about birth control methods, it is possible to deduce from some of the respondents' replies that they had been faced with unplanned pregnancies. Third, although many returned to their studies on a part- or full-time basis after they had started to work, the longer a man was away from his studies, the harder it was to return to them.

While many were resentful that they had to interrupt their studies to earn money, not all of them felt that this had been a negative experience. Some found that the work which they did had a positive effect on their later career development by helping them to specify their occupational choice and by providing them with work experience on which they could build. Several reported that they were motivated to go back to school or to change their career planning because they were so dissatisfied with their first jobs.

We are now in a position to summarize what we have learned about the way in which our group prepared for their careers. First and most conspicuous is the finding that for those who sought to prepare themselves for a scientific or professional career the road was very long. Most of the group did not complete their formal preparation until their late twenties or early thirties and a significant minority took even longer.

The first choices which they had to make were centered around their education, later around the challenges of adulthood. They had to decide upon a major in college, whether to go on to graduate school, in what field to concentrate, and whether to study for a doctorate. At some time they had to meet the challenge presented by military service; they had to decide whether to marry and at what age, when to start a family, and whether to complete their studies and then seek a job, or reverse the process, or attempt both simultaneously. Sometimes their options were considerable; at other times they were severely restricted by circumstances that were not under their control. But the majority of our group convey the impression of having been in substantial control of their career development. For most of them, not even marriage or children forced an alteration in their career goals.

Beneath these generalizations, considerable variability existed. Some who acquired a doctorate early also managed to marry and start a family early. Others who acquired a wife and children early, however, failed to earn their doctorate. Apparently some had the ability and energy to do everything—to acquire a doctorate, wife, and children— and to do it quickly. But others who married and had children while they were young did not seem able to cope with these added responsibilities and at the same time complete their work for their doctorate.

Much the same dichotomous situation is revealed with respect to the age when the respondent took his first full-time job. Some who got their doctorates early were able to start to work while they were still quite young. But others who started to work full time when they were young never succeeded in getting their doctorates.

Our data do not enable us to unravel the dynamics underlying these and other relationships. Two speculations, however, are in order. The first suggests that included in our group was a significant minority of very able and energetic young men who could meet the challenges of career, war, and family life and work out solutions which enabled them to get a running start on life. Others who married, had children, and accepted full-time employment before they had completed their education were unable to combine these challenges successfully. Their new responsibilities, no matter how personally rewarding, interfered with their career planning so that they had to alter their occupational goals, sometimes radically.

It may be well to remind the reader of some of the conventional beliefs that were called into question by the data which we have just reviewed. We did *not* find that:

A large proportion of young men complete college without knowing what they want to do;

Teachers have a considerable influence on the occupational choices of their students;

Most students take a disproportionately long time to acquire their doctorates;

Military service is a seriously disruptive influence on the career planning of young people;

Those who serve on active military duty acquire their doctorates more slowly than those who do not serve.

Early marriage is a serious deterrent to a man's acquiring a doctorate.

All of these propositions appear reasonable. But none was supported by our data. The factors involved in career development are subtle and must be analyzed in depth.

5

# Patterns of Career Development

Much more is known about the way in which young people prepare themselves for work than about their experiences after they begin to work. There are, however, several pieces of information concerning career development which are in the common domain. A very high proportion of certain groups such as physicians, who have pursued a long period of training, are likely to remain in their professions throughout the whole of their working lives, while others who have also pursued professional or technical training such as lawyers, engineers, clergymen, scientists, often shift out of the field for which they were originally trained. Some may even never enter their chosen field, such as the lawyer who goes into an administrative post in government upon graduation from law school, or the chemist who upon receiving his master's degree accepts a position with the marketing division of a large corporation.

Although considerable data have been assembled about the occupational mobility of those who have had advanced education, the information is usually gross and reflects shifts among occupations or jobs. Very little information is available about the more subtle but important changes within the same field, such as when a physician shifts his role in a hospital from therapist to administrator, or when he changes the nature of his employment and leaves his own practice to work for an industrial firm or a government agency. Moreover, since most occupational studies are limited to reporting job changes, they do not consider the interaction of forces within the individual and within the world of work that lead some to continue in the same work and others to make moderate or even radical changes in their careers.

This chapter will attempt to describe systematically the first ten to fifteen years in the work history of our group and determine the varying degrees of continuity, shift, and change that occurred in their occupational development. In developing this description attention will be devoted to three dimensions of the process: the direction, progression, and continuity of the individual's work history.

With respect to *direction*, the question is the relationship between the individual's present work and his original occupational goals. Are the two identical or closely related or was the individual deflected from the route on which he had set out so that it can be said that he changed direction?

Since jobs are hierarchically ordered and since even very able and well-prepared persons usually begin at or close to the bottom rung of the ladder, an important axis of occupational analysis is the extent to which the individual moves up the ladder over a period of years. Is his career development characterized by an element of *progression*?

A third facet of the way in which men enter into and make their way in the world of work relates to the number and degree of interruptions that they experience. Some move from their entrance job straight ahead while others may be deflected because of military service, family demands, or a decision to return to school. The element of *continuity* is a third important dimension of career development.

We will now attempt to order the occupational experiences of the members of the group in a manner that will reveal parallels and differences in the direction, progression, and continuity of job experiences. Our aim is to develop a limited number of discrete patterns of occupational development. Although we will eventually want to explore the range of internal and external forces that may be associated with each of the discrete patterns, the task of this chapter is to order the occupational materials on a phenomenological basis. The search for causative factors to explain these patterns will have to await the introduction of additional data, particularly those relating to the levels of achievement and the value orientations of the members of the group.

The likelihood that we will uncover career patterns is increased by the fact that many sectors of the world of work are rather rigidly structured. The conditions for employment and advancement are more or less explicit, and the hierarchy of positions is generally known. Although the conditions governing promotion may vary from one institution to another and even within the same institution, most of those who enter upon and engage in the competition for better jobs are likely to acquire early a reasonably clear idea of the performance required of them if they are to advance.

There are some sectors in the world of work which are not rigidly structured. Advancement in such professions as architecture, journalism, engineering, and many others is relatively open. There is even less structure in some sectors of business, government, and self-employment. But here too there are discernible tracks. However, individuals may be deflected and therefore we cannot know in advance which individuals or how many in a particular group will reach the higher levels in the occupational hierarchy. At best the patterns can provide the framework within which to study the differential work history of individuals.

While the environment within which the members of our group made their decisions contributed to the establishment of certain occupational patterns, the heart of these patterns is imbedded in the cumulative decisions which the individual makes about the successive alternatives that he confronts. It must be emphasized again that as a result of their excellent preparation and the favorable economic conditions during the period when they were starting out on their careers the members of our group had a wide range of options.

The number of discrete patterns that we could delineate would depend both on the variability of the career development of the group and on the analytical use that was to be made of the patterns after they had been elaborated. In view of the basic character of the study, which was exploratory and would seek to open up key questions rather than to provide exhaustive answers, we decided to limit ourselves to three basic patterns.

The first characterizes those individuals whose career development follows a more or less straight path; after they have crystallized and specified their occupational choice, they enter and remain in one field and continue to perform essentially the same type of work. Among those who follow this pattern is the young man who selects chemistry as a major in college, goes on to earn his doctorate in chemistry, and then enters an industrial laboratory, where he remains;

or the individual who in college chooses journalism as a career, becomes the editor of the college newspaper, attends a graduate school of journalism, and then takes a job as a reporter and continues to hold down positions as a working journalist. We define this type of career development as a *straight pattern.*

Related, but clearly distinguishable from those in a straight pattern are individuals whose career development reveals that they have shifted their field or have moved to perform a different function within the same field or have made both changes. The key word that describes this group is "shift." Their new field or the new functions that they perform in the same field are more or less logically related to what they had been doing before. There is no sharp break between the new activity and the old. The type of shifts involved suggests that these individuals have broadened their occupational horizons by extending and expanding the range of their interests and activities.

Among those who fall within this second pattern is the young man who earns a doctorate in economics and starts his career as a college teacher, but leaves this position after a few years to become the economist for a bank where he thereafter is concerned primarily with economic research and writing; or the engineer who on graduation accepts a job in industry but after a few years returns to the university to take a doctorate in physics. He then joins the faculty of a school of applied science where he teaches and conducts research in advanced electrical engineering. Those whose careers are characterized by such proliferation and shifts are said to follow a *broad pattern.*

The occupational histories of those who fall into the third group, which we have designated as the *variant pattern,* are quite different from the other patterns and differ among themselves. First, they contain individuals who have made one or more radical changes in their field of activity, such as the geologist in our group who after a few years of college teaching went into a retail business. Those whose careers are marked by such radical changes resemble to some degree those who fall within the broad pattern, except that their careers contained radical changes rather than moderate shifts both in direction and continuity.

The other major subgroup that falls within the variant pattern is composed of individuals who have not altered the direction or continuity of their work but whose careers reflect a lack of progression. They have advanced not at all or very little. They are related to those in the straight pattern except for this lack of reasonable progress. This group includes, for instance, the young classicist who ten years after earning his doctorate is still an assistant professor, a position which he has held for eight years. Although he has moved from one institution to another he has not moved up the academic ladder. Another example of those who follow the variant pattern is the talented young man who takes a job as a high school teacher to support himself while he attempts to write a novel. But the novel remains unfinished and he remains in this position.

Since the occupational development of the group was characterized by directedness and persistency, it is not surprising that 58 percent of the group falls into the straight pattern. However, the proportion comprising the broad pattern is surprising. In view of the favorable intellectual endowment and advanced education of the group and the favorable employment situation, we might have anticipated that the proportion which fell into the broad pattern, which was 29 percent, would have been higher. Of course time is a factor here. If this group were reappraised a decade hence, it is likely that the proportion in the straight pattern would be smaller, that in the broad pattern larger.

The relatively small size of the variant pattern, 13 percent, might have been expected. Since one criterion for this classification was a lack of progression in their career development, it is not surprising that only a minority of these able people followed this pattern.

Our classification scheme could be applied to a wide range of occupations as well as to those represented by the members of this group. For instance it would be feasible and probably illuminating to study the occupational histories of a group of skilled workers or a group of clerical or sales workers in terms of these three patterns. But while the schema might have broad applicability, the distributions which we found to prevail in the present study might not apply to other groups. Members of our group had a long time to try out and test their interests and capacities; they had to make a great many decisions about their education and training such as whether they were willing to invest time, effort, and money in preparing for particular careers. They were therefore much more likely to be deeply committed to their choices than would a group of clerical or sales workers whose education and training had been much less extensive and who had not made corresponding sacrifices and commitments for the accomplishment of a specific career goal. Moreover the members of our group were in a better position to shift or change their career goals because of their superior endowment and training than occupational groups with less training who would have been more limited in their alternatives.

The following extracts from the questionnaires indicate the criteria that we used to distribute the respondents among the three career patterns. A member of the American foreign service used language identical to our own to describe his career development and he is thus the prototype of those who fall within the straight pattern. "I have followed a more or less straight line since my senior year in college as regards choice of career and pursuit of it. . . . The fact that I chose active employment with the federal government is a consequence of the opportunity following college to have an introduction to a career along these lines. . . . I derive great personal satisfaction from my work. Let us say simply that I chose the right career for me and am happy with my work and the future it offers."

An attorney on the West Coast also hewed to a straight path. "My choice of profession has always been the law. It has been a very rewarding and absorbing profession. I have thoroughly enjoyed my training for and the practice of my profession, as well as the associations and opportunities it presents." Not even five years of military service deflected him!

A professor of music reported the stages of his career development as follows: "At 7 introduced to music through piano lessons. After reaching a decision at 12 to become a composer my parents and the schools which I attended made possible lessons in piano, theory, history of music through 'released time.' Good choice of a university (with School of Music) helped. A small legacy at the end of the conservatory years made it possible for me to come to New York and then pursue studies with [a major contemporary composer]. . . . So far as the 'compositional career' rather than the academic career is concerned, fellowships . . .

made it possible to get away from teaching at intervals and obviated the necessity to teach summer school."

An assistant professor of classical languages dates his career development from high school: "Foreign languages, especially Greek and Latin, have greatly interested me from secondary school days. I majored in Latin and Greek at B——— College . . . with a view to becoming a college teacher. I continued my work in classics at Columbia University where I received the A.M. and Ph.D. degrees. Since leaving Columbia, I have embarked on a career in college teaching."

These cases illustrate the type of career development followed by those whom we included within the straight pattern. They are individuals who usually were headed in a particular direction by the end of college if not before, and they moved along the same track through graduate school and work, from one decade to the next.

The special quality of their occupational development that we sought to capture through the use of the word "straight" is further isolated when we contrast them with those whose careers fall within the broad pattern. This second group includes an international consultant in mining resources. His early employment was in engineering in connection with various mining enterprises. He returned for two years of graduate study in mineral economics because his job experience had pointed to the significance of this field. During the next five years he was employed as a mineral economist by corporate and governmental agencies. He then became the executive vice president of a uranium company but left shortly thereafter as a result of a disagreement with the president. He then became a consultant for both private companies and governments. Five years ago he

accepted a position with an international agency in which
he is presently employed. This man's career development
is the result of a broadening of interests, capacity, and responsibility. Each step in his occupational history is meaningfully related to his previous experience and in turn lays
the foundation for the next step.

A group leader in statistical analysis in a research and
development laboratory on the West Coast got his first job
after high school in 1942. "Though I had taken a college
entrance course, finances did not indicate a college education. Our small school did not promote scholarships. . . .
I did take a science talent exam and received honorable mention. Incidentally, though I was interested in civil engineering I wrote an essay on guided missiles and rockets, not
dreaming that one day I would be working on the design of
moon and planetary space craft. My mother pushed me to
enter college . . . and by part time work in a cheese factory (3 to 7 a.m.) . . . plus my mother's sacrifice I received
a B.A. in civil engineering in February 1946." After he was
awarded a fellowship by Columbia, "the direction of my
career was altered upward. I turned down a position to stay
at Columbia after receiving my M.S. in favor of returning to
[my undergraduate college]. Had I stayed at Columbia my
career would undoubtedly have been different. After teaching until 1952, I married. I knew I needed experience or
a Ph.D.—I had turned down the latter opportunity by
not staying at Columbia. Since my wife had asthma and
I wanted aircraft experience, the logical location was
California."

He became a stress engineer at a major aircraft company
but soon was dissatisfied. "Through a friend who worked
in a space laboratory I learned of a possible opening. I

applied with no immediate indication of success. A month later, however, I received a job offer. Thus I arrived at the laboratory and the present level of my career."

Here is a case of very considerable broadening. At first college was beyond his horizon; then graduate school seemed outside his purview. But in each case the leap was made. While he did not earn his doctorate, he was able to secure first a teaching position at the college level and later a research position in a space laboratory. From arsenal worker to development engineer represents a substantial broadening!

A young veteran with a liberal arts degree had an opportunity to join the staff of the prosecutor at the war-crimes trials that were held some years after World War II. After several years on this staff, he left to pursue graduate work at Columbia. From 1950 to 1955 he held a position as an instructor in government at a good college. After securing his doctorate, he joined the Department of State as Intelligence Research Specialist. Again the several stages of a career are related to each other and this respondent's present work is the natural outgrowth and extension of both his education and his earlier work experience.

In contrast to those in the straight pattern who are on a single track, those in broad pattern tend to move away from their original locus or focus. However, the direction towards which they move is related to their previous work. It is an outgrowth of earlier experience. The past, present, and future are organically connected. They frequently manifest an element of venturesomeness or eagerness for the new in their approach to their work.

Even though the number of the respondents who fell into the variant pattern is relatively small, they represent a particularly interesting group because of the difficulties that they experienced in getting launched on their careers despite their substantial ability and superior education. An illustration of this group is a highly successful member of the bar, a partner of a firm that carries his name, who noted that "after being a working newspaperman for four and a half years I wanted a more permanent and financially remunerative way of life . . . therefore I went through law school and became an attorney. I have found now both the permanence and the remuneration that I sought."

Another respondent had also started work as a journalist and continued somewhat longer before he changed to another field. He had been a newspaper writer for four years and then became the editor of a trade association magazine. As an outgrowth of this job he "found an opportunity to increase income through a marketing practice" and established himself as an independent marketing consultant. He then took a further step and became a part-time lecturer in marketing at a large university. At the time he replied to the questionnaire he had been promoted to associate professor, but his teaching was still limited to a part-time schedule. In this case we can see how the change came about. Through his editorial work the respondent became acquainted with a new field. From journalism to marketing and teaching represented a complete change rather than a broadening of occupational goals, since his new occupation had no similarity or relation to his former one.

A radical change in field and function but not in employer characterizes the career development of a research chemist who became a patent expert. After graduate work in chemistry he accepted a position with a large industrial corporation in laboratory research. At the time he replied

to the questionnaire he was working in the patent department. In the interim he had moved from a city in up-state
New York to New York City which both he and his wife
greatly preferred. After relocating he had attended law
school at night and graduated. This change in his career
"required considerable thought." The considerations that
led him to it were: "1) In industrial laboratories, research
projects in physical chemistry tend to be ancillary to primary projects in organic chemistry or physics; 2) In the
lab, the opportunities for supervisory experience were very
limited—lab technicians were seldom available to research
chemists with less than five years experience; 3) Major interests and abilities . . . did not favor a shift in emphasis to
research in organic chemistry; 4) While working in the
laboratory I found my ability to analyze and write up research results were above average. This is important in
patent work."

In the foregoing instances, the respondents made radical
changes in their careers and landed on their feet; in fact,
they improved their circumstances and prospects. Of course
they might have been in a better position had they earlier
had a clearer perception of their needs and desires and of the
realities of the world of work. But confronting work situations that were unsatisfactory relative to alternatives which
they had not previously known about or had not considered,
these men were able to mount the considerable effort of
making a radical change and are doing well in their new
careers.

Others who made changes, however, did not really solve
their career problems. They continued to find considerable
dissatisfaction in their work. For instance, a respondent who
is currently a self-employed lawyer reported a modest in-

come of between $5,000 and $7,500 annually. His original training had been in chemical engineering, and he had been employed for several years in this field. This is how he summarized the change in his career: "Interest in chemical engineering work was my own. However, after having been released twice due primarily to economic factors, I was a proper subject for the influence of an uncle who was a practicing attorney. As a result, I obtained my law degree. . . . Occasionally I feel a sense of longing and nostalgia for the engineering field, but I feel it is getting too late in life for any further changes."

One of our respondents had been a radio announcer for several different stations for four years. Then, for a brief period, he became the associate editor of a fairly successful new monthly magazine. He left this job and returned to radio announcing. He then tried high school teaching for one year but did not like that. In 1960 he joined a West Coast paper as a feature writer. He reported a salary of $5,800 per year and stated that he expects to stay with the paper until retirement. Here is a case of much movement but little progress.

The common characteristic of this group within the variant pattern is a belated or unsuccessful resolution of occupational choice. While some are able to crystallize or change their choice by making special efforts later in their lives and do not suffer serious set-backs, others are not able to make such an effort or cannot do so successfully. In many instances where such a difficulty exists it appears that an underlying personality problem is finding expression in the occupational area.

Our attempt to order the work histories into a few basic patterns pointed up the continuity and consistency characteristic of the occupational development of most of the group. In general, even those who did not stay with their original choices entered fields which were organically related to their previous experience rather than grasping an accidental opportunity.

We cannot expect to understand what might account for these differences in the career development of our respondents by looking for a single factor. The case materials have suggested a great variety of determinants in the choices and decisions that the respondents have made about their work. In looking for the differentiating characteristics our first line of inquiry is to search the preparatory process. Were there significant differences in the age at which they crystallized their occupational choice? The answer is an unequivocal yes: there were differences and they were pronounced. Over three-fourths of those in the straight pattern had determined on their occupational goal before college graduation, while only two-thirds of those in the broad pattern and just over half of those in the variant pattern had crystallized their choices by this time. At the conclusion of their graduate studies only 2 percent in the straight pattern, 4 percent in the broad pattern, and 24 percent in the variant pattern had not reached a resolution of their occupational choice.

An inspection of the grades which the respondents received in graduate school was also revealing. The largest proportion of the graduate students with the best grades (A and A+) were found in the straight pattern, the smallest proportion in the variant pattern. Correspondingly, those with the lowest marks in graduate school were more likely to be in the variant pattern than in the straight pattern.

There was one rather subtle matter with respect to grades

that warrants mention. Slightly over one-third of those in both the straight and broad patterns had pursued fields of specialization in graduate school in which the departments did not grade routinely. Doctorates were awarded on the basis of oral and written examinations alone. But the percentage of those in the variant pattern who followed courses of study for which grades were not given rose to 57. There is a possibility that the relatively unstructured nature of their graduate education intensified the problems connected with crystallizing career objectives for those who later fell into the variant pattern. However, it is also possible (at least we cannot exclude the possibility) that their choice of these fields of study itself reflects some element of uncertainty, hesitancy, or doubt about occupational plans.

Another important differentiating characteristic of the respondents within these patterns turned out to be the earning of a doctorate and the age at which it was received. More than 3 out of 4 of those in the straight pattern achieved this degree; 69 percent of those in the broad pattern, but only slightly over half of those in the variant pattern, received the doctorate. With respect to age, those in the straight pattern were more likely to receive their degree relatively early, and those in the variant pattern were concentrated among those who received it late.

The explanation of these findings remains somewhat equivocal; we cannot be sure whether the speed with which those in the straight pattern acquired their doctorate helped to anchor them occupationally or whether the early clarification of their goals enabled them to pursue their doctorate aggressively. There are also alternative lines of explanation for those in the variant pattern: was it their uncertainty about their occupational goals that reduced the proportion of those who acquired a doctorate or delayed those who acquired it; or did the lack of this degree handicap their later occupational development? While our data do not enable us to select the correct hypothesis it is possible that these alternatives are not mutually exclusive.

To what extent does a period of military service and the length of service help to differentiate among those in the three patterns? Sixty-five and 62 percent respectively of those in the straight and broad patterns served on active duty, and a somewhat smaller percent (53) of those in the variant pattern saw military service. Possibly more of the variant group were rejected for military service on psychological grounds. While approximately one-quarter of those in the straight and broad patterns served for less than two years, only about one-tenth of those in the variant pattern served for such a short period. This longer military service of those in the variant pattern may have had an adverse effect on their career development.

An interesting finding about length of service is that the highest proportion serving four or more years was found among the broad pattern. There is a strong presumption that during such a lengthy interruption, many men reappraised their original plans and considered how to make use of their military service so as not to "lose" four or more years. Apparently a considerable proportion found the answer by broadening their careers in a manner which enabled them to make constructive use of what they had learned in the military.

A third line of inquiry about the career patterns involved such differentiating characteristics as the fields, functions, and institutional settings in which the respondents worked. Among the questions to be explored were these: were there subtle ties between each pattern and the field or functions in which the respondents worked, in that some fields and functions helped to lock people in and therefore kept them in a straight pattern, while other types of work facilitated broadening their development? Are the career patterns perhaps no more than a disguise for these basic determinants?

With respect to fields, those with careers in the natural sciences are overrepresented in the straight pattern, and those in the humanities and business are overrepresented in the variant pattern. With regard to the broad pattern, the fields are fairly evenly represented except for a slight overproportion of those in engineering. A few speculations can be ventured although definitive answers cannot be provided. The relatively high proportion of those in the straight pattern found in the natural sciences can be explained by the fact that without a high degree of directedness and perseverance one is not able to qualify for a specialized career in science; a high proportion of those who pursued their education to the doctorate in a scientific field were likely to be strongly attracted to this type of work, and the opportunity to be well rewarded in science probably encouraged many to stay with it.

The high proportion of those in the variant pattern who were following careers in the humanities or business may reflect the difficulty for one trained in the humanities to find a satisfactory alternative if he becomes dissatisfied with his original choice and the appeal of business for those who do not have or cannot maintain strong professional interests.

The relatively greater proportion of those with a broad pattern who had studied engineering may reflect the fact that engineers in large profit-making organizations often have a good opportunity to move over into general management where the financial emoluments are greater. The choice of engineering in college often reflects a mixture of scientific and economic interests, and this may explain why many engineers later broaden their occupational horizons.

With regard to the relations between the functions performed by the respondents and their career patterns, the following emerged: there was overrepresentation of those in the variant pattern in teaching alone, of those in the straight pattern in teaching and research combined, and of those in the broad pattern in administration. As might be expected, the following underrepresentation emerged: the broad in teaching alone, the broad and variant in teaching combined with research, and the variant in research and research administration.

A few comments on the foregoing: teaching alone seems to have been too restricted for those who sought to broaden their occupational goals, while it helped to provide a refuge for those still in search of a final resolution of their career problems. Teaching combined with research, which is usually a preferred university position, was secured most readily by those who had developed excellence in a particular discipline. Research and research-administration were beyond the range of those in the variant pattern, who had not acquired sufficient depth in a particular discipline. Administration was a magnet for those who wanted to broaden their careers, and it offered an escape for some who had initially floundered.

A few interesting findings emerge from a consideration of the career patterns and the institutional settings within which the respondents worked. There was overrepresentation of the straight pattern in academic life, of the broad in corporate enterprise, and of the variant among the self-employed. These findings are easy to interpret. A high proportion of graduate students start their careers as teachers in the subject of their specialization. Many in the straight pattern started in academic life and continued in it. Those in the broad pattern, however, sought to expand beyond their starting point and found preferred opportunities in corporate enterprise. Some started in business with the intention of broadening out if and when the opportunity offered.

The overrepresentation of the variant among the self-employed is probably a composite result: some who were uncertain about their future sought to avoid an institutional commitment for as long as possible, others had tried and failed to fit themselves into a hierarchical structure, and a few were pursuing lines of work such as writing or composing in which they could be on their own.

We see then that the career patterns are to some degree characterized by the field, functions, and institutions of the work of the respondents; but since the statistical differences are not very pronounced, other factors are unquestionably present and operative.

There is one more piece of evidence at hand. This derives from the answer to whether the patterns can be distinguished in terms of the average number of employers worked for by the members of the group. The findings are surprising. Almost 3 out of 5 in the straight pattern had worked for only one or two employers; this was true of 26 percent of the broad and only 19 percent of the variant. Most of those in the broad pattern had had three or four employers. Almost half of those with a variant pattern had had five or more employers while only 9 percent of those in the straight pattern had had this many. From the explanations they offered about job changes we know that those in the broad pattern used employment opportunities that opened up to expand their occupational horizons and goals. The frequent job changes of the variant indicated that these people did not like what they were doing and hoped that they would fare better if they shifted to a different field or function or institution. The infrequent job changes of those in the straight pattern do not in general reflect absence of opportunity but rather a disinclination to make a change which might deflect them from long-run career objectives.

The data presented above about the preparatory cycle and several facets of the work experience of the members of the group suggest that the career pattern scheme, although it was developed on the basis of gross occupational behavior, was actually associated with the personal characteristics and probably with the total personality structure of the respondents. Otherwise the many connections which we found between the patterns and the other factors in their career development could not be explained. It may be helpful to pull together what we have learned about these factors which appear to be associated with the career patterns.

Those in the straight pattern appear to have a stronger commitment to their occupation than those in the other patterns. For the most part they resolve their occupational choice early, and once they enter full-time work they tend to remain set. They stay with one employer or make only a few shifts. They convey the impression of having a good capacity for work. Many had very good grades in graduate school and a high proportion secured their doctorates.

Those in the broad pattern appear to be less committed to a specific field. They take a somewhat longer time to decide on their occupational choice and, having decided, they seem less firmly bound to it. Their somewhat looser interest in a particular field of work is probably reflected as early as graduate school where their marks tend to be less good than those received by individuals in the straight pattern. They were apparently able to adjust to long military service, sometimes even to build on it. They tend to work for more employers and generally seem more fluid with respect to their career development. As a group, they convey the impression of being in search of a goal beyond a particular job, i.e., they are more readily deflected from their original course. Additional data suggest that they may also be more responsive to outside influences.

The most conspicuous characteristic of those in the variant pattern is that they experienced difficulties in resolving their occupational choice. Some crystallize a choice only to find after a time that they are dissatisfied with it and that they must tackle the problem anew. Others are simply stymied from the start and struggle for a long time to find a satisfactory resolution without much success. They do less well in graduate school, and a considerable proportion of them are not accepted for military service. A high proportion do not acquire a doctorate. When they go to work, many take up teaching as interim employment; others prefer to be self-employed. Those who work for others change employers frequently, apparently in the hope that their next job will prove more satisfactory than their last. The variant pattern conveys the impression of many able people who have experienced difficulty in coping with the world of work, possibly because they cannot meet these demands and at the same time cope with the other demands that are made on young adults. But included in the variant pattern are others who have considerable strength. They realize, usually fairly early in their careers, that they have made an initial mistake in the determination of an occupational choice. But they face up to this and make the necessary adjustments. Many do much better the second time around.

The career patterns thus turn out to have significance on several distinct levels. Descriptively, they tell us about the occupational history of our group. If we compared the patterns of our respondents with those of another sample —graduate students of lesser ability or people who stopped their education earlier, it is probable that significant differences would be found in the career development of the two groups. The patterns also have value as an analytic tool which enables us to explore connections between the career development of individuals and various forces in the occupational world that influence and affect them. They also provide a basis for precipitating an analysis of certain personal characteristics that find expression in the occupational area.

For our purposes the career patterns have provided us with a first opportunity to order the diversified materials which reflect the occupational experience of this talented group during the early years of their careers. We can say that the patterns of career development tell us something about the groups of individuals within them. At this point we do not know what a pattern can reveal about a particular individual, since it is a gross category reflecting only broad tendencies.

Finally, of the three constituent elements—direction, continuity, and progression—the patterns are most revelatory about the first two. Only in the variant pattern, and then only with respect to some of the group, was the lack of progression a key characteristic. The role of progression in a career still remains to be examined in its own right.

# 6

## Measures of Success

During the years this investigation was under way, many who heard about it inquired, "How well did the talented do?" "Were they successful?" "How many fell by the wayside?" This interest in the level of accomplishment or achievement of the group is understandable, because everybody is curious about the extent to which individuals with talent eventually fulfill their promise. Moreover, there is a great deal of interest in the factors that may explain why some do well and others poorly. Just beneath the surface of American democracy and egalitarianism there is a suspicious and withholding attitude towards gifted people. This is associated with a Puritan outlook that considers work, perseverance, and dedication the only important virtues which justify being rewarded. Since accomplishment based on endowment seems to be effortless, it is sometimes felt that it does not deserve special rewards.

Aside from the distortions that might easily be introduced as a result of intellectual and moral preconceptions, the systematic analysis of the achievement of a group of talented persons was bound to be complex. When we decided to undertake the analysis by developing rather gross categories, we knew that such an approach would have costs as well as advantages. We realized that it might obscure important answers to important questions. But an overambitious effort would almost certainly fail because there are not enough guidelines in earlier studies.

We might have decided to compare our group, with its heavy preponderance of men who had earned a doctorate and were currently engaged in teaching and research, with another with the same educational and occupational characteristics, differing only with respect to whether they had been awarded a fellowship. But this would have contributed more to an appraisal of the fellowship procedures than to our understanding of the success of talented individuals. We did, however, undertake a comparison between the income level of our group and that achieved by much larger professional and scientifically trained groups, and from this gross comparison we were able to conclude that the members of our group had done quite well.

We believed that there was more to be learned, at least initially, from a more thorough appraisal of the relative success of different subgroups among our talented sample and by including a broad range of factors in such comparisons. No single factor can tell us much about the important subjective aspects of success wherein men measure their accomplishment not by a comparison of their income with that of others, but in terms of how well they have met the expectations and goals which they had initially set for themselves.

While we are concerned with both dimensions of success —the social and the individual, or the objective and the subjective—the aim of this chapter is restricted to developing a series of objective measures which can be used to assess the differential levels of achievement of various subgroups within our total sample. In seeking an answer to this basic question of how well these men did in their chosen fields, we used five criteria: income, rank, responsibility, quality of employing institution, and personal reputation. Income is the most generally useful standard for measuring "success" in our society since it is the only standard that permits easy comparisons among members of different occupational groups and members of the same group in different sectors of the economy. Still it has limitations: average salaries and the range of salaries vary among occupations with the same educational requirements; they vary from sector to sector within the same occupational field; and it is often difficult to ascertain the true income of individuals in the same or different fields or institutional settings.

A word about each of these limitations. For several decades those with advanced education in the sciences and the social sciences have been able to command a higher average salary than those in the arts and the humanities. Moreover, the earnings of those who reach the top in business or in self-employment are greater than the earnings of those employed in universities or government. During the 1950s the gap among the sectors widened; business was in the best position to adjust its salary levels upward in response to both the underlying inflation and the relative shortage of trained personnel; government and colleges lagged behind. The last decades have seen the elaboration of fringe benefits, which makes it even more difficult to arrive at a realistic measure of income already complicated by the fact that many academicians use the summer to earn additional income rather than devoting it to study and research.

We sought to take account of these variations by establishing different income criteria for the same levels of achievement in the different sectors of the economy. But we found it desirable to move beyond income and to take other factors into consideration in assessing a man's achievement.

Rank is clearly indicative of the status that an individual has been able to achieve within the organizational setting in which he works. His status can be further delineated by evaluating the responsibilities that attach to the position which he holds. These include such factors as his role in the decision-making process, the number of people under his supervision, and the extent to which the work he performs has a bearing on the future of the enterprise. The standing of the employing institution is another significant variable: the dean of an Ivy League college has arrived at a level of achievement quite different from that of the dean of a small state teachers' college.

In a few instances one additional piece of information was used—the fame or reputation of the individual as reflected in special acknowledgement that had been made of his work by competent judges. For instance, a national or international award is certainly relevant for the determination of the achievement level attained by an artist.

We had considered the much more subtle approaches used by Professor Kenneth Clark of the University of Minnesota and Professor Donald MacKinnon of the University of California to measure the accomplishment or success of talented persons whose careers they were studying. They, as well as others, have relied on developing a consensus among experts in identifying and evaluating contributors to a field. There were two practical reasons that we could not use such an elaborate method. First, we were studying a group with a work experience of between ten and fifteen years. Therefore only a relatively small proportion were likely to be well known to the leaders in their field. Second, we were studying not one group, such as Professor Clark had done when he surveyed the accomplishments of psychologists, nor even a few groups, such as have occupied

Professor MacKinnon's interest, but almost the entire spectrum of occupations for which graduate and professional
study is essential or preferred preparation.

We therefore developed a schema predicated on three
*levels of achievement* among which all of the respondents
were distributed: upper, intermediate, lower. We had
already developed a fivefold category scheme which enabled
us to classify the institutional settings within which people
worked: academic, nonprofit, government, corporate, and
self-employed. Since the role of income relative to other
rewards varied from one setting to another, more weight
was given to monetary rewards for those employed in
corporate enterprises and for the self-employed, and to rank
and responsibility for those who worked in an academic,
nonprofit, or governmental setting. A few illustrations can
help to illustrate the method which we followed in making
our classifications.

A teacher who held the rank of full professor in a major
institution and who earned at least $10,000 per year was
placed in the top achievement level. But we did not place
in this achievement level a corporate employee or a self-
employed person unless he earned at least $20,000. A research
or staff professional in corporate enterprise with substantial
responsibility, however, was placed in this achievement level
if he earned at least $17,000. For individuals employed by
nonprofit or governmental organizations, more weight was
given to the significance of the work they performed and
the responsibility they carried. An income of at least $15,000
was used as an indication that an individual in such an
institutional setting was holding a key position and those
with this income were classified in the upper level.

Similar adjustments were made in setting the parameters
for the intermediate level. Relatively few problems arose in

classifying the respondents. The principal difficulties involved determining whether a few individuals belonged in the upper or the intermediate level and whether a few others belonged in the intermediate or the lower.

A few more examples will indicate how the respondents were classified. All of the following group were placed in the upper level: a professor of chemistry at a leading university in the Midwest whose salary was $10,700 for the academic year; a group supervisor in mathematical research in an applied physics laboratory whose annual salary was $20,500; a professor of economics at one of the Big Ten universities whose academic salary came to $12,500; the owner of a chemical manufacturing firm in the Southwest who indicated that his income was "sizable" and who had left a well-paying position with a leading chemical concern to go into business for himself and reported that he had substantially increased his income; a tax analyst for a West Coast utility company who earned $17,800.

Those who were placed in the intermediate level included: a professor of industrial engineering in a technical institution whose academic salary amounted to $9,600; a consultant in engineering and economic evaluation on the staff of a large chemical company who earned $16,000 annually; a professor of organic chemistry at a polytechnical institution whose annual salary amounted to $9,300; the chairman of the department and professor of sociology at a women's college earning $10,000 per annum; a foreign service officer of the Department of State with a base salary of $11,660.

Into the lower level were placed the following respondents: an assistant professor of zoology at one of the Big Ten universities with a per annum salary of $8,000; a senior development engineer at a nonprofit scientific laboratory on the West Coast who earned $11,000; an associate professor of geology at a university in one of the Mountain states whose academic salary was $8,000; the feature writer for a leading Western newspaper who earned $5,800 per year.

In our classification scheme, then, we used an elastic measure of income as a criterion of success and relied heavily on the importance, significance, and responsibility that attach to the work performed by members of the group. Our classification scheme is at once more qualitative and more sensitive to the relative rates of progress of able people in quite different occupations and institutional settings than a scheme based solely on income differentials. The use of income ranges to discriminate among achievement levels in different work settings was particularly important since more than half of the entire group were employed in academic institutions where throughout most of the postwar years salaries lagged behind other sectors of the economy.

Since the primary objective of our classification system was to facilitate a comparison of the relative achievements of the members of our group, the lines of demarcation among the three levels could be relatively arbitrary. We decided to establish roughly equal groups.

Table 6 shows the relationship between achievement levels and current income.

TABLE 6. *Achievement level and income, in percent* (N = 342)

| | *$10,000 under* | *12,500 $10,000–* | *14,999 $12,501–* | *$15,000 over* | *unknown* |
|---|---|---|---|---|---|
| Achievement level | | | | | |
| Upper | 9 | 36 | 31 | 76 | 13 |
| Intermediate | 30 | 42 | 57 | 24 | 38 |
| Lower | 61 | 22 | 12 | 0 | 49 |
| Total | 100 | 100 | 100 | 100 | 100 |

The table reveals that despite the several adjustments which we made there remains a strong positive association between income and achievement level. Only a small percent (about 1 out of 11) who earned less than $10,000 were placed in the top achievement level, and only 1 in 4 who earned over $15,000 was not placed in that level. The median income was about $15,000 in the upper level, somewhat over $11,000 in the intermediate level, and under $9,000 in the lower level.

The amount of money that people are able to earn and their achievement in terms of other occupational criteria depend in some considerable measure on their age, since the length of time they have been in the labor market is a factor of their age. Because we did not take age into consideration in establishing our categories, we explore in Table 7 the relationship between achievement levels and the age of the respondents.

TABLE 7. *Achievement level and age, in percent* (N = 342)

|  | Present Age | | | | |
| --- | --- | --- | --- | --- | --- |
|  | *31–36* | *37–39* | *40–42* | *43–45* | *46 or older* |
| Achievement level |  |  |  |  |  |
| Upper | 20 | 40 | 28 | 44 | 38 |
| Intermediate | 32 | 35 | 44 | 27 | 34 |
| Lower | 48 | 25 | 28 | 29 | 28 |
| Total | 100 | 100 | 100 | 100 | 100 |

Several points emerge. As might be expected, those in the youngest age group are overrepresented in the lowest achievement level. This reflects at least in part the fact that they have not been at work for a sufficient number of years to have moved up the occupational hierarchy. Since the older age groups tend to be slightly overrepresented in the upper level, we can see that age *is* a factor in achievement. However, the relatively high proportion of the 37- to 39-year-old age group in the upper level indicates that many men can move towards the top in a few years.

But age masks other functions of the passage of time. An equally important question is the number of years that an individual has been able to work effectively. This requires an allowance for interruptions brought about by military service, illness, pressing financial need, and other types of career disturbances and interruptions. These are taken into account in Table 8 by adjusting for "time lost."

Two comments can be made. Those in the youngest age group are still overrepresented in the lower achievement level, but after some point—approximately ten years at work—additional years of employment do not affect achievement significantly.

As noted earlier, more than half of the entire group was engaged in teaching or research where professional advancement requires a doctorate. To what extent did a doctorate determine achievement level and furthermore how significant for later achievement was the age at which it was acquired?

Table 9 indicates that it is more probable that individuals who did not acquire a doctorate would be in the lower level.

TABLE 8. *Achievement level and corrected age, in percent* (N = 342)

|  | Corrected Age | | |
|---|---|---|---|
|  | *27–35* | *36–41* | *42 or older* |
| Achievement level |  |  |  |
| Upper | 26 | 36 | 38 |
| Intermediate | 31 | 39 | 35 |
| Lower | 43 | 25 | 27 |
| Total | 100 | 100 | 100 |

It also appears that those who acquired a doctorate early were more likely to be in the upper level.

The tables presenting the relationship between age and achievement levels point to the following conclusions. A man must spend at least a certain number of years in his profession before he can reach the higher levels. Those who have only recently begun to work and those whose work has suffered many interruptions are more likely to be

TABLE 9. *Achievement level and age at earning doctorate, in percent* (N = 342)

|  | Age at Doctorate | | | |
| --- | --- | --- | --- | --- |
|  | 22–27 | 28–36 | 37 or older | no doctorate |
| Achievement level |  |  |  |  |
| Upper | 49 | 31 | 28 | 32 |
| Intermediate | 30 | 41 | 46 | 26 |
| Lower | 21 | 28 | 26 | 42 |
| Total | 100 | 100 | 100 | 100 |

found in the lower achievement levels. After a certain length of time at work, additional years are not likely to increase markedly an individual's chances of raising his level of achievement. Those who intend to pursue an academic or research career are more likely to succeed if they acquire a doctorate and especially if they can do this early.

In addition to these general findings that achievement differentials in our group are not simply a function of age or time spent in pursuit of a career, there are four bodies of data—family background, educational accomplishment, military service, and work experience—that might throw some light on the level of achievement of the respondents.

With regard to family background, the key determinant is the occupational level of the father; this carried some rough indication of the family's income and educational status.

Table 10 indicates a positive, though not very strong, correlation between the achievement level of our respondents and the occupational level of their fathers. On the basis of supplemental information we find that a higher percent of the respondents with foreign-born fathers were in the higher achievement levels than were those with native-born fathers. Apparently these immigrant families, despite the problems engendered by their relocation, provided a home environment more conducive to the development of their offspring, characterized as it was by a higher educational, cultural, and income status; these parents may also have encouraged their children to strive harder.

TABLE 10. *Achievement level and father's occupation, in percent* (N = 279)

|  | Father's Occupation | | | |
| --- | --- | --- | --- | --- |
|  | professional and white collar | proprietors and managers | blue collar workers and farmers | unknown |
| Achievement level | | | | |
| Upper | 40 | 26 | 23 | 0 |
| Intermediate | 28 | 40 | 41 | 83 |
| Lower | 32 | 34 | 36 | 17 |
| Total | 100 | 100 | 100 | 100 |

Those respondents who themselves had been born abroad were more likely to be in the two higher achievement levels. Among the native-born respondents, those from New England were conspicuously underrepresented among the upper achievement level.

It would require much more data than we assembled to

sort out the differences in parental circumstances that may have exercised an important influence on the achievement level of the respondents. In particular, it would be desirable to have information about changes in family circumstances between the birth of the respondents and the completion of their education. An incisive analysis would also require knowledge of the interpersonal relations in these families and how the members of our group responded to the values and goals of their parents. From the data at hand, we can make only a rough assessment of whether the family's objective circumstances were more likely to assist or to retard their children in acquiring a higher education.

As noted earlier, we had only indirect information about the religious affiliations of the respondents and then for only about 70 percent of the group. Within this group we found that Protestants were more likely to be in the two higher achievement levels; that Jews were concentrated most heavily in the intermediate level and, like the Protestants, were less likely to be found in the lower level. Catholics were heavily represented in the intermediate and lower levels. A cross-check revealed that a higher proportion of the Catholic respondents came from homes in lower socioeconomic levels. Neither Catholic nor Jewish respondents gave any indication that they had been discriminated against either during their educational preparation or in employment. This does not necessarily mean that they had completely escaped discrimination, but it did not appear to them to have been an important factor in their career development.

One broad generalization can be distilled from the foregoing. The data point up that while those born into the better educated and well-to-do families were more likely to be in the higher achievement levels, many who came from less favorable family circumstances were also able to rise to the top achievement level. The son of an educated and high income earning father is likely to have an edge, but a considerable number whose fathers had little education or money were able to reach the top through their own talent and efforts.

While there is a close link between family background and the type of higher educational opportunities to which one has access, other factors such as residence, scholastic ability, the availability of scholarships also play an important role; they often determine the type of college that a young person is able to attend, and this too can have an influence. Those who attended large state or private institutions under religious sponsorship or institutions which specialized in technical curricula were more likely to be in the top achievement level. Those who attended Ivy League colleges (other than Columbia) or who attended other academically strong private colleges were significantly overrepresented in the lower achievement levels. What lies back of this unexpected finding of the poorer performance of men from the stronger colleges is hard to determine. It may be that at that time the stronger students from those institutions went directly into business or entered professional schools at other universities, or that the fellowship committees at Columbia gave preference to applicants who had attended these "prestige" institutions and possibly accepted many with lesser potential.

We have some data which show whether undergraduate honors were associated with achievement level. These results also are contrary to what one might expect. Those who had graduated with honors, had won medals or prizes, had been elected to Phi Beta Kappa, were somewhat more likely to be in the lower two achievement levels than in the top level. Those who reported that they had been awarded a scholarship or other type of formal recognition for scholastic excellence and those who had been elected to an honorary academic fraternity or society were no more likely to be in the top achievement level than those who did not report any awards. A third set of data tends to reinforce the foregoing. Those who had received no undergraduate honors or distinctions of any type were more likely to be in the top achievement level than those who had been singled out for recognition.

To explain these paradoxical results we must once again resort to speculation. Often undergraduate honors are awarded to students who tend to do well across-the-board. It may be that many of these honor students are not deeply committed to a particular field or again that their broad interests are associated with a lower order of creative power; therefore they eventually do less well in the field of their specialization. We must also consider the possibility that those who were more successful in their careers reported less fully on their undergraduate achievements.

It appears then that undergraduate performance, at least for our group, is a poor criterion of later achievement. But there was a definite relationship between graduate performance and later achievement.

Those with the highest marks in their graduate courses were more likely to be in the top achievement level and least likely to be in the lowest achievement level. Those with a B average, as well as those whose work was not graded, were more likely to be in the lower achievement levels. We should note, however, that despite this association between grades in graduate courses and later achievement, a considerable minority who did undistinguished

work in a graduate or professional school did reach the top
achievement level, as shown in Table 11.

TABLE 11. *Achievement level and grade average in graduate
courses, in percent* (N = 342)

|  | Grade Average | | | |
|---|---|---|---|---|
|  | A+/A | A— | B range | no grades |
| Achievement level |  |  |  |  |
| Upper | 46 | 36 | 31 | 26 |
| Intermediate | 38 | 33 | 33 | 36 |
| Lower | 16 | 31 | 36 | 38 |
| Total | 100 | 100 | 100 | 100 |

We found in the files kept at Columbia letters of recom-
mendations written about the respondents, mostly by their
professors in graduate school, which we compared with
their later performance. Those who had been rated by their
teachers as having above average abilities do not show up
disproportionately in the top achievement level. Those who
were considered to have outstanding personalities, however,
were likely to be in the top achievement level. Those who
were considered to have above average abilities together
with an outstanding personality were the most likely to be
found in the top achievement level. This suggests that
eventual success, even in intellectual pursuits, depends on
more than intellectual ability alone. An interesting sidelight
on these professorial evaluations is the fact that men who
were considered by their teachers to be "colorless" were
much more likely to be in the lower achievement level than
those whose personalities had been assessed as "unattractive."

We can now introduce some further data which may shed
some light on the differential performance of the members
of our group. The number of years that students spend in
acquiring their doctorate affects the level of achievement

that they can reach during the early part of their careers, since in many fields they cannot advance without a doctorate. We have two pieces of information that bear on this point: the number of years that elapsed between the respondent's securing his bachelor's degree and his acquiring his doctor's degree, and the number of years between his acquisition of his doctorate and the time we collected our material.

Those who earned their doctorates in a short time, within five years after receiving their bachelor's degree, were much more likely to be in the top achievement level. Those who required between six and eleven years to earn the advanced degree were most likely to be in the intermediate level. The slow group, those who acquired their doctorate twelve or more years after their bachelor's degree, were more likely to be in the intermediate or lower achievement levels.

The advantage of moving expeditiously to acquire a doctorate is indicated by Table 12, which sets out the relationship between the number of years since the respondents received their doctorates and achievement levels.

TABLE 12. *Achievement level and number of years of work experience after doctorate, in percent* (N = 245)

|  | Years of Work Experience | | |
|---|---|---|---|
|  | *1–5* | *6–11* | *12 or more* |
| Achievement level |  |  |  |
| Upper | 15 | 35 | 44 |
| Intermediate | 27 | 42 | 39 |
| Lower | 58 | 23 | 17 |
| Total | 100 | 100 | 100 |

How was military service, and particularly the length of military service, related to later achievement? Our data show that those who did not serve were somewhat more likely to be in the top or intermediate achievement level. Somewhat surprising is the finding that those who served for one year or less were much more likely to be in the intermediate or lower level. This may reflect the fact that the Armed Forces tended to discharge individuals who were ineffective in the service before their normal tour of duty would be over. Some with short service probably fell into this category. Those with four or more years of service were overrepresented in the top achievement level. This may reflect to some degree the finding noted earlier that many of these men with extended military service had succeeded in building their careers on their military experience.

Those who served only in the enlisted ranks were found to be more heavily represented in the intermediate and lower achievement levels, while those who started as enlisted men and then became officers were more heavily represented in the intermediate and upper achievement levels. Those who served only as officers were more heavily represented in the top or intermediate achievement level. Thus the different levels of military accomplishment are clearly differentiating with respect to later performance; officer status was strongly predictive of later higher achievement.

How can we account for these positive relationships between military rank and later achievement? All of our group had the intellectual capacity to qualify for officer status, but apparently some did not want to serve as officers and others were judged to be unsuitable. Although there are of course marked differences between military and civilian life, there are also significant parallels. The men who succeed in either area are likely to have many characteristics in common, including the motivation to do well wherever they may be.

Those who served as officers had an opportunity to acquire certain valuable experience. Their selection for officer training and successful performance as officers may have increased their self-confidence, which together with their greater experience gave them an advantage in civilian life.

The disproportionate number of those who had no military service who were also in the top or intermediate achievement levels would seem to contradict these findings. However, the explanation of this apparent contradiction may be found in the fewer interruptions to their careers and perhaps also by the experience that they gained in civilian war work.

The age at which the respondents first entered upon full-time employment turns out to have a significant relationship to achievement levels. Those who began to work relatively early, before they were 25, were more heavily represented in the upper achievement levels, while those who had their first full-time job later were more heavily represented in the lower achievement levels.

The concatenation of circumstances leading to high level achievement seems to favor individuals who came from middle class homes, who did very well in graduate school, who earned their doctorate early, who served as officers in the military service or did not serve at all, and who started full-time employment before they were 25. Others succeeded, but the odds were more heavily weighted against them.

Additional information enables one to relate employment experience to achievement levels. These additional data relate to the field, the nature of the functions performed in work, the type of employers, and the number of employers that characterize our group.

Table 13 sets forth the relationship between major occupational field and achievement level.

TABLE 13. *Achievement level and occupational field, in percent* (N = 342)

*Occupational Field*

|  | humanities | social sciences | natural sciences | engineering | business | professional |
|---|---|---|---|---|---|---|
| Achievement level | | | | | | |
| Upper | 23 | 33 | 34 | 31 | 36 | 67 |
| Intermediate | 29 | 39 | 37 | 55 | 32 | 23 |
| Lower | 48 | 28 | 29 | 14 | 32 | 10 |
| Total | 100 | 100 | 100 | 100 | 100 | 100 |

The markedly high proportion of independent professionals in the top achievement level probably reflects the tendency of the more successful to work for themselves or in a partnership while the less successful were more likely to shift into salaried employment. It also reflects the relatively high incomes earned by able professional men during the 1950s. The disproportionately large number of those in the humanities in the lower level may indicate that this field offered fewer opportunities for rapid advancement, and that here it was harder than in the social or natural sciences to combine teaching with more remunerative large-scale research and consultation. It is also noteworthy that there is no significant difference between those in the social and natural sciences from the point of view of achievement; there is no clear advantage to one or another scientific field.

Table 14 sets forth the relationships between achievement level and fuctions performed.

The ablest academicians are likely to combine teaching

TABLE 14. *Achievement level and type of work performed, in percent* (N = 342)

## Type of Work

| Achievement level | teaching | teaching and research | research | research and administration | administration | staff | professional |
|---|---|---|---|---|---|---|---|
| Upper | 25 | 41 | 10 | 50 | 48 | 26 | 50 |
| Intermediate | 33 | 34 | 50 | 45 | 33 | 30 | 31 |
| Lower | 42 | 25 | 40 | 5 | 19 | 44 | 19 |
| Total | 100 | 100 | 100 | 100 | 100 | 100 | 100 |

and research, just as the ablest people in industrial research are likely to acquire administrative responsibilities. Both groups are overrepresented in the higher achievement levels. Similarly, there is strong competition for administrative jobs which tend to carry the higher rewards in our society. Hence, those who succeed in becoming administrators are more likely to have reached a position and salary that characterizes the top achievement level. Younger men are likely to hold staff jobs; older men who remain in these jobs may have somewhat less motivation or competence which is likely to be reflected in a lower achievement level. Teaching alone and, interestingly, research alone are not the roads to success—at least not according to the criteria which we used.

The data did not reveal a close relation between the institutional setting in which the respondents worked and level of achievement. This was partially because in establishing our categories we had already adjusted income. There was a slight tendency for those in corporate enterprise to reach only the lower achievement levels; this may reflect the fact that so many of our people were in technical rather than line positions. There was a tendency for the self-employed to be more successful; a high proportion of them were in the top achievement level.

This brings us to the last aspect of the employment story; the relation between job mobility and achievement. Here the differentiations are considerably sharper. Those who had worked for only one or two employers were more likely to be in the higher achievement levels; among those who had worked for more than two employers, the trend was towards the lower achievement level; the same is true for those who had made still more job changes.

We might have assumed that those who had worked for many employers were more likely to be in a higher achievement level since they were actively searching to improve their positions. And this explanation may well fit the minority who were in the top achievement level and who had had five or more employers. But most of those who changed jobs frequently appeared to be less concerned with their occupational achievement than with a continuing search to "find themselves." They may have been running away from work and jobs that they did not like, not seeking out those which would speed them up the occupational ladder. And it appears that the many who remained with their original employer or changed employers only once did so not because of lethargy, but because they were satisfied with their original decision and career development.

The employment facets just discussed reveal that a self-employed professional or a person who combines two functions, such as research with teaching or with administration, and who finds a favorable institutional setting and remains within it is more likely to be successful.

Let us now see whether the categories of career patterns, which included an element of progression, are independent of the achievement categories.

TABLE 15. *Achievement level and career pattern, in percent* (N = 342)

|  | Career Pattern | | |
|---|---|---|---|
|  | straight | broad | variant |
| Achievement level |  |  |  |
| Upper | 34 | 39 | 20 |
| Intermediate | 38 | 37 | 24 |
| Lower | 28 | 24 | 56 |
| Total | 100 | 100 | 100 |

Several findings are contained in Table 15. An individual who has followed a straight or broad career pattern is less likely to be in the lowest achievement level. However, we do not know whether he will be in the top or intermediate level. If he has a variant career pattern, he is much more likely to be in the lowest achievement level. The two category schemata are substantially independent: some in the variant career pattern landed in the top achievement level. Thus we can conclude that the element of progression included in our definition of career patterns is substantially independent of the measures of success developed in the present chapter.

The following is a profile of one most likely to attain a high level of achievement according to the findings developed above. His father is a professional man or holds a managerial position; he attended a religious-sponsored or technical college; he had very high grades in graduate school; he was assessed by his professors as intellectually strong and with an attractive personality; he earned a doctorate expeditiously; he served in the Armed Forces as an officer; he is able to combine in his work two or more functions such as teaching and research or research and administration; he finds a suitable institutional setting and avoids many job changes.

Our analysis of achievement so far has been grounded exclusively in socially objective criteria. It is time now to consider the important subjective determinants, particularly a man's values and goals which go far to give direction and meaning to his occupational strivings and accomplishments.

# 7

# Value Orientations

We have introduced two of the three major analytical axes which we have established to describe and evaluate the data that we collected for the study of talent and performance. In constructing the career patterns we sought to organize and evaluate the behavioristic materials which describe the successive stages in occupational development. In constructing the achievement levels we sought to order and distinguish through the use of social criteria the rate of progress made in careers. Each approach enabled us to bring some order out of the largely inchoate mass of data.

But each approach had the same limitation. Each considered almost exclusively the decisions and consequent actions taken by the members of our group at various stages of their career development as reflected in categories conventionally used to describe social behavior, such as the number of years an individual attended school or how many times he changed jobs. Except for our occasional deductions about what may have been back of these decisions, these approaches did not consider the individual himself.

But if the analytical framework is to be adequate to the subject our scope must now be broadened to include the individual. We now must attempt to assess the forces that lie back of and give direction and meaning to the decisions that men make with respect to work and work-related activities. For the individual is not passive in the structuring of his career however much he may be buffeted by forces beyond his control. While external forces may overshadow the self-directing efforts of people who do simple work for which they need little specific training, this cannot be assumed with regard to our group who spent over twenty years preparing for work.

The basic question then is not whether to broaden the framework to make room for the individual but how to do it effectively. While we cannot hope to encompass all aspects of the individual's personality, we must at least elucidate the basic preference systems that underlie the choices which he makes with respect to his work and career.

The major elements of an individual's preference system can be described in terms of his needs, goals, and values. A word about each. Every individual has needs, wishes and desires, and some are so powerful that he must seek to gratify them directly and quickly. But no adult is restricted to or bound completely by his immediate needs. He has other goals, long-range objectives which he has set for himself. Their particular quality is that they have a time dimension and cannot possibly be achieved immediately. Hence they provide a link between the present and the future; the future goals determine the behavior in the present which is directed toward their realization. We make a distinction between needs and goals because individuals must frequently defer the satisfaction of some of their needs in favor of accomplishing some long-range goal.

Values, the third constituent of the individual's preference system, may demand postponement or renunciation of the search for satisfaction of various needs; sometimes they are actually at variance with some of his needs. On the other hand, values have the power of needs in determining an individual's behavior. Values are evolved during the course of the individual's development as he accepts some and rejects others from among those which are strongly held by persons close to him and by the society in which he lives. It is this dual origin of the adult's value scheme which accounts for the fact that it may be at variance with the dominant values of his society. Another source of variability is the diversity of value orientations held by various subgroups in the larger society.

Values are the generalized principles to which the individual has committed himself; in turn these help him to choose and order the alternatives that he encounters in any number of life situations. Since individuals hold more than one value, there are frequently pulls and counterpulls among them. The individual then must organize his values into some type of system, loose or tight, by arranging them into some sort of hierarchy. The elaboration and organization of such an ordered system of values is a major developmental task of the individual during adolescence and early adulthood. When he has established such an order, he can handle more readily any situation involving choices in terms of values which are more important and others that are less important to him.

Different individuals evolve significant differences in attitudes towards work. An artist may spend months on one painting, while a businessman may devote evenings and week ends to working out a merger. Although they both devote their major energies to their careers, neither has much understanding of the values of the other. Each may even look with suspicion on the work of the other.

We need not consider such sharply contrasting careers to illustrate the wide differences in attitudes towards work. They also show up among individuals who appear to be pursuing much the same type of work. Take the college science teacher and the research scientist. The teacher is likely to find his major satisfactions in the classroom, in his relationships with his students whose horizons he seeks to broaden and whose competences and interests he hopes to deepen. He is engaged in an ongoing exchange with a group of young people whose intellects and personalities are still in the process of development, a process that he seeks to direct and influence.

The research scientist may find his greatest peace and contentment in his laboratory, alone with his chemicals and apparatus. One of his major needs and desires may be to establish a wide no-man's-land between himself and others, for he does his best work and derives his greatest satisfactions when he can think uninterruptedly in abstract terms and then test whether he is on the right track.

The individual's preference system which is, as we have seen, composed of his needs, goals, and values, determines his choices in all aspects of his life, including the choices which he makes initially, and then again and again in the area of his work. Since out of the complexity of their endowment and life's experiences, individuals develop different preference systems, and since as a result of their educational and employment experiences, they confront a wide range of work situations, it is inevitable that wide differences exist among people in what they seek from their work and their careers. This diversity, embedded in the differences among people and within the range of opportunities that prevail in the world of work, is increased by changes that are inevitably introduced with the passage of time—as the individual grows older and as the economy and society are altered.

The large number of different attitudes that prevail toward work and career in a modern industrial society confronts the investigator with the challenge of developing a system of classification that is both valid and practical. The way in which people approach their work, their career objectives, the satisfactions that they seek to derive from their work—in short, the whole web of their occupational objectives—do not stand alone. They are part of a larger nexus which encompasses what the individual hopes to get out of life itself—his total life values and goals. The underlying preference systems are the spine which give structure to these larger dimensions.

It was difficult to develop a category scheme that would enable us to assess the role of values in work and career. First, a quantitative approach would not allow for interaction among values; second, each individual's value hierarchy is to some extent unique; and third, we wanted to relate an individual's principal values to other aspects of his life. We resolved these difficulties by deciding on a highly simplified approach. We evaluated each case in terms of what appeared to us to be his dominant value orientation, disregarding subsidiary aspects of his value scheme as well as the sometimes highly personal coloring that it might assume in any given instance. Finally, we focused our attention primarily on those values which had a direct bearing upon work.

In reviewing our cases we were struck by the fact that several respondents saw their occupational development largely in terms of resolving acute value conflicts. Such was

the young man with a socialist background who after earning his doctorate in philosophy sought to make his living
by working with his hands. But he also wanted to make use
of his education and training. For many years he was torn
between these two values. He finally resolved his conflict
by reconciling his intellectual interests and ambitions with
his equally strong desire to make a humble contribution
to the welfare of others. The latter could be considered
his dominant value orientation. In most of our cases, however, there were no such conflicts, and we were able
to discern without difficulty the dominant value orientations
that appeared to have a guiding influence on the individual's
attitudes and decisions concerning his work.

We developed a fourfold system of classification. We
considered individuals who had a distinctive value orientation toward work as belonging to one or another "type,"
but our categories were arrived at empirically and do not
reflect any preconceived social or psychological theory.

The first and most striking value orientation is held by
people whose attitudes and behavior towards their work are
characterized by a strong desire to structure their own
activities and to be as free as possible from any pressure or
interference from others. Underlying this attitude is a deepseated desire to pursue their own interests. These individuals
also want to make optimal use of their capacities in their
work. They want to be in a position where they are free
to set and change the objectives which they pursue. They
want to set their own pace at work. They desire as much
freedom as possible to determine their relations to their
collaborators and their colleagues. Above all, they want to
be free from directional dictation.

The common denominator in these attitudes is the

strength of their need or demand for a high degree of autonomy in their work. This is the all-pervasive factor. When such a person is confronted by a choice, the consideration that looms highest is how his decision may affect the degree of autonomy that he exercises in his work. Because his behavior with respect to his work is so much under the dictate of this search for individual autonomy, we have called a member of this group the *individualistic type*.

The orientation of the second group towards work is focused on their relations to others in the work situation rather than, as in the case of the individualistic type, on subject matter or on materials. Those in the second group are much more heavily involved in the organization or structure within which work is carried out, and even more specifically in their hierarchical relationship to the many other individuals and groups who play a part in the work process.

Among the needs and desires that the members of this second group display in their attitudes and behavior towards their work is a strong drive to direct and guide the work of others. They share with the individualistic type a strong aversion to being directed and guided by others. But their response is quite different. They do not flee from people, but they do not want to take orders from others. They seek a leadership role and they feel comfortable and happy when they are in a position to encourage others, in one fashion or another, to follow the directions which they have established. In broad, their objective is to control others and their work. Some of this group are content with a supervisory role where they serve as the source of information, encouragement, and correction; they do not want to control minutely the work of others. They want those who work for them to recognize that they are the source of authority and power, but they do not need to demonstrate constantly to those under them that they do in fact possess such authority and power. Some of this group, however, are not content unless they can demonstrate repeatedly that they are dominant.

The keynote to the behavior of this group is their desire for authority over others, not, as with the individualistic type, autonomy for themselves. Achievement for these people is to arrive at a position of dominance over others. They can be, and frequently are, just as deeply committed to their work as the individualistic type. But their efforts are directed towards securing, holding, and expanding their positions of influence or dominance over others. They are in search of positions of leadership, and for this reason we decided to call them the *leadership type*.

The third type is concerned neither with optimizing their freedom of choice nor with dominating others and aggrandizing their own power. Their basic orientation is to gain, hold, and increase acceptance by other members of their work group. Among their main characteristics is their desire for security and satisfaction which they derive from membership in a work group or larger organization. They find satisfaction in being able to meet the demands and expectations of the group to which they belong. It is the esteem and approval of the group that is at the heart of what they want from their work activities. They are group- or community-minded persons. They feel good about being a member of "the team." They have a tendency to conform to the mores and attitudes of the group, an orientation that has been subsumed under the caption of "the man in the grey flannel suit." These people are more at ease if they do not have to work alone. They have no objection if another person issues orders and supervises their work; in fact they may prefer it that way.

This type stands in sharp contrast to the individualistic type; they freely and willingly give up the "autonomy" which the others prize so highly. They also differ from the leadership type who seek separation from the rest of the work group in order to dominate it. The group-oriented individual seeks to lose himself in the group. The fulcrum of his relationship to his work is the magnetism that the group exerts on him and his desire to be bound more closely to it. Hence, we have called him the *social type*.

The outstanding characteristic of the members of the fourth group is their dedication to a system of social, religious, or political ideas and ideals. While they may be interested in and involved with groups in their work, they are primarily concerned with ideas or ideals which they seek to propagate and advance. Their goals are to serve a higher value—higher in that it transcends their own needs and wishes. They seek the acceptance, sometimes by small numbers, more frequently by many, of a set of ideas and ideals which they hold to be true and worthy of dedication. Their own needs and wishes tend to get pushed into the background, as they become enmeshed and involved in furthering their causes. Their work takes on the quality of a "calling" as they attempt to proselytize for a religion, a revolutionary political doctrine, or some other overriding end. Most, though not all, of these individuals tend to make a commitment to a cause early in life, and they often, though again not always, stay with it for the rest of their lives. Since their work is directed by an overriding commitment to a set of ideals or ideas, we have designated these individuals as the *ideological type*.

The ideological type frequently shares one aspect of the orientation of each of the other types, but differs from them in others. For instance, the ideological type frequently seeks autonomy, but his search for autonomy is not for himself but for the cause for which he is working. Ideological types are frequently engaged in leadership struggles, but they want power over others not for itself but because they sincerely believe that power is essential to furthering their cause.

While the ideological like the social type is concerned with relations to the group, there is an important difference. If a conflict should arise between loyalty to the group and loyalty to the ideology, the ideological type has no difficulty in turning his back on the group and remaining faithful to his ideology. Even during the Nazi holocaust which showed all too clearly the power of the group to command the allegiance of its members even at the cost of their having to betray previously held values, the power of conviction enabled ideologically oriented individuals to resist group pressures. Those who hold deep political, religious, or moral convictions and commitments may become exiles, members of a resistance movement, or even sacrifice their lives. For centuries, believing Jews, offered the choice between conversion and death—a choice which Hitler did not offer —chose death. Such was the depth of their religious commitment.

The ideological type may think that the individualistic type is too concerned with private matters, that the leadership type is too concerned with power for its own sake, and that the social type overvalues the group *qua* group because he does not concern himself with the ends that the group seeks or represents.

These four types are not of course as mutually exclusive

as our schematic description might suggest. Some individuals have many of the characteristics of the individualistic type and still have elements of the leadership, social, or ideological types. This is true of each group. Nevertheless, while it was difficult to classify certain respondents we were able finally to subsume each of them under one of our four types.

The following quotations indicate how the respondents were classified according to the dominant value orientations which were reflected in their work and career development.

First is a profile of an individualistic type who is currently an associate professor of geology and senior research scientist.

I did not get along too well with my father and this gave me a drive to get ahead on my own. I am an only son and I spurned my father's good-income business ($25,000) to work on my own for much less money.

I decided not to marry because the personal responsibility might have forced me to leave my chosen work.

[Under what conditions would you leave your present position?]

Those providing an opportunity in change of living and working conditions or if political pressures would become too unbearable here.

[What is the least gratifying aspect of your work?]

In part editorial work, but mostly personnel management and relationships with petty officials, self-appointed dictators, and supersensitive colleagues.

I used to work every day and every evening. I now often relax on Sundays and don't work more than two nights a week.

[What do you plan to do after retirement?]

Continue with my research, perhaps write or rewrite a textbook.

A successful government research scientist, also classified as an individualistic type, added the following comment to his questionnaire: "You are interested in the conservation of human resources. Well, the greatest conservation measures you can devise is to foster a climate in which creative people are free to pursue their own goals, untrammeled by stricture of money, institutional rigidities, red tape, pedantics, choking critics, and group conformity. I accept limits, of course, but where are they?"

A quite different outlook towards work is suggested by the following two summaries of the careers of men who were classified as the leadership type. The first is a general manager of a subsidiary of a large chemical company. He left his previous position because of an "interest in broad management responsibility," and he accepted his present job because of his "interest in being associated with a well-financed, research-oriented, progressive company." He would leave his job if an "opportunity to totally manage a technically oriented larger new business arose." He explained that he had "changed from research to research management and general management in an effort to exert overall control on outcome and fate of my own work." He anticipates over the next decade that "additional responsibility will come with probable rapid growth of the area of business responsibility." He finds most gratifying "the task of organizing new activities with capable, intelligent workers and associates." His additional activities include "professional society, Junior Chamber of Commerce, Kiwanis," and all sorts of manual and skilled crafts, which he describes as an "excellent change of pace leading to more effective human performance." He contemplates that after he retires he will do "consulting work or start [my] own

business." In assessing the factors affecting his career development, he notes as "interfering" factors: "1) disinterest
in people; 2) impatience with co-workers."

The second example of the leadership type is a professional man who had recently shifted from the successful
practice of the law to a senior position with a large lumber
concern with gross sales of over $35 million annually. He
explained his shift in these terms: "In the course of my
practice . . . I began to feel frustrated because the power
of decision always rested with the client, as well as the
rewards (or other consequences) of the cause of action
selected." As the most gratifying aspects of his present
work he referred to "being in the line of command rather
than in an advisory position as a lawyer." He shortly expects to "assume complete responsibility for the operation
of my present company as it becomes the wholly owned
subsidiary of a larger corporation." He expects that in ten
years he will be "president of a major corporation" and in
twenty years "chairman of a major corporation."

The chief design engineer of an important durable goods
manufacturing concern typifies the social type. Among the
situations which might lead him to leave his job, he listed
"an adverse change in my superiors that would lead to un-
pleasant human relations." In looking back over his earlier
jobs he concluded that his "development was not systematically planned and executed by my superiors." Contemplat-
ing his future progress he said, "I do not know the specific
nature of that advancement but it is at least five years away
and management will make the decision according to the
needs of the company." Among the least satisfying aspects
of his current job, he singled out, "not enjoying consistently
full conifidence of my superior." He listed among his addi-

tional activities: "homeowners' association, gardening, home maintenance, contributing to children's education." The first factor he cited as interfering with the growth of his career was "lack of guidance from superiors." In an additional comment he laid further stress on the strategic role of his superiors in his development: "The greatest disappointment in my professional career was the realization . . . that most fruitful knowledge comes from doing rather than from being taught by others. I found most superiors either consciously withholding information or technically too weak to educate others, or just not caring."

Another example of the social type is an associate professor of English who listed the following explanations for taking a series of academic positions:

Eastern University: Opportunity to serve my teaching apprenticeship at a first-rate eastern university.
Southern College: Opportunity to teach interesting courses in a quality institution in a colorful city.
Preparatory School: I liked teaching in a first-rate preparatory school in New York City.
Chairman, High School English Department in A_____:
I felt drawn by the challenge of working to help a small "typical" community.

The following is his listing of the most gratifying aspects of his work: "1) The satisfaction of working with young people at a malleable, responsible age; 2) The pleasure of working alongside congenial colleagues in a congenial intellectual atmosphere; 3) A sympathetic department head who seems to understand and appreciate my special interests and abilities." His additional activities included playing the organ in church at Sunday services, other church work, serving on committees, as an usher, playing the piano, interior decoration. His father had been an influential Methodist clergyman in the South and the respondent said that he expected to retire at 65 after which "I should like to take a house in London and live among the English for the rest of my life."

Illustrative of the ideological type is the philosopher, mentioned earlier, who wanted to work with his hands. He is now an associate professor of philosophy, a position he reached only after a detour of about ten years. In the middle of his graduate studies in philosophy, he left the university to live and work "among the people" as a machinist, artist, teacher, and in still other occupations. In 1957, he returned to the university to complete his work for the doctorate and to pursue his academic career which he had interrupted on ideological grounds.

"I was torn between intense and sincere interest in philosophy and the notion that my social and political commitments required more direct involvement in life (with a big L) than academic life afforded. Philosophy, I believe, had to be functional, and ethical and social values needed more than philosophical analysis; they needed functional fulfillment. Dewey and Marx convinced me, as did a radical upbringing. I must add that my years in the art field, and as a machinist, were not frustrating with regard to the work I was doing. . . . I enjoyed working at a machine, I enjoyed working as an artist. It was not intrinsic dissatisfaction with the work that led me to make a major change back to academic life. It certainly wasn't money, which I have always been weak-minded about. But it was a positive sense of waste, and an intellectual frustration—I *needed* students and colleagues—contrary to the post-graduate notion that I could be a nonacademic philosopher that led to the decision. My point here is that it is *not* particularly frustrating for

*this* Ph.D. to do manual or technical work for a living . . .
The absence of fulfillment of one's training rather than the
promise of attractive kinds of work" held the key to this
respondent's dissatisfaction. He saw "two apparently mutually exclusive considerations: 1) self-fulfillment in terms
of a major early investment in direction of work; 2) social
(or other) obligations which preclude this self-fulfillment.
The resolution is to discover that they are not mutually
exclusive . . . but they need to be constantly and continually reviewed, Aye, there's the rub."

In explaining why he had taken certain types of work, he
indicated he "wanted to do manual labor, prospective union
activity (idealistic?)." His additional activities included
"cultural and political organizations . . . these activities in
some cases contributed to my sense of social obligation, my
interpretation of the role of a teacher in society."

There were others who had less difficulty in resolving a
conflict between an ideological commitment and a choice
of a field of work. Included in the ideological group were
several missionaries, one of whom had responsibility for
supervising a very large school system in the Congo; another had worked in the Far East among the Japanese.
There were several Catholic priests pursuing careers as college instructors and a Protestant minister with an urban
church. Still another example of an ideological type was a
foreign service officer who said, "I decided early that, for
me, satisfaction from my work . . . would be derived from
the feeling of importance which could be attached to my
work. . . . World War II and its aftermath . . . led me
inevitably to focus upon foreign policy as the area of greatest importance. . . . I am, I suppose, what can be described
as an 'idealist'."

We had no difficulty in assigning any of the foregoing

into one of the four types that we had established to differentiate among value orientations as they relate to work. It was more difficult to assign a classification to those who had conflicting values. For instance, there was a physician on the staff of a government hospital who is currently the head of the metabolic unit on the medical service. "I think that the main problem facing me at this crossroads is a materialistic one—living at the level which is 'expected' of a maturing physician, providing security for young children, maintaining a home—in general, providing all the 'goodies' of a materialistic society on a $15,000 income. Society pays substantially for services, not much for thought, teaching, research, or government work. If one's chief goals and pleasures lie in these areas one must reconcile oneself with falling behind in the economic competition. While one can easily make the decision for oneself, the dictates of family responsibility make the choice much more difficult."

An associate professor of physics who "had contemplated dimly the idea of the ministry" while on a fellowship at Cambridge, England, wrote that "this idea has recurred from time to time, stimulated by a desire to commit my life wholly to the service of Christ (the logical inescapable consequence of becoming a Christian) and balanced by a feeling that this service lay in academic life as a layman, rather than in the ministry. Despite my enjoyment of, and satisfaction in, the work, both teaching and research, and despite what seems to me to be a fair talent in this line, I have been feeling more and more dissatisfaction with it both in terms of the demands it makes on the physicist's life and in terms of the irrelevance to man's major needs . . . The primary motivation for pure research is at the root of its curiosity, and the pursuit of it seems like self-indulgence, at least in the present day, when the scientific and technical advances we have already made have been so little applied to meeting the world's needs. These general considerations then . . . have led me to consider such a change. It seems to be impossible now, but it is nonetheless much on my mind."

There were others who were caught between conflicting values, but rarely did the conflict cut so deeply and the resolution loom so difficult as for the two described above. We classified the physician as an individualistic type, for though he fretted about his relatively small earnings he continued to pursue the type of work he preferred. We included the physicist with the ideological types because even though he had continued to work in physics, his concern with finding a way of practicing his faith appeared to be compelling in the shaping of his life.

Although the types we delineated were developed on the basis of the case material in this study—that is, they were constructed from the value orientations of highly endowed and educated individuals, they appear to have wider applicability. For instance, we could easily find people of the individualistic type among those who pursue such disparate careers as farmers, truck-drivers, storekeepers, skilled workers, handymen, taxi drivers, and still others.

The leadership type is likely to be in many fields besides corporate enterprise. Wherever power is concentrated at the top of a hierarchical structure such as in politics, trade unions, the Armed Forces, even in the church, the universities, hospitals, men with the characteristics of the leadership type will be competing for power. However, the nature of competition in closed institutions results in a rapid thinning of the ranks of the leadership type near the top. Many who start are unable to tolerate the adjustments they must make in order to advance and at the same time to avoid drawing the hostility and the opposition of competitors on themselves. Only those with very deep leadership needs and a range of capacities are likely to reach the top or near the top.

In the work force at large, the greatest number are probably the social type. Work to them is a mixture of the good and the bad; they enjoy it but they also resent it. Much of their work satisfactions derive from the social context within which their work is carried out. They make friends at work and enjoy the companionship of many with whom they are less closely tied. They do not intend to become a boss and they have no desire to be their own boss. They see their work as a key part of their lives but they see it primarily as a job that yields income. We pointed out years ago in *The Unemployed* (1943) that the major deprivation attendant on losing one's job and not finding another is the cost of social disenfranchisement. The unemployed man has no place to go in the morning, no place to spend the hours of the day, nothing to return home with at the end of the day.

The ideological type may be more rare in an affluent society than in other societies. For instance, the Catholic Church has long found it necessary to recruit manpower from abroad to run its schools, hospitals, and other basic institutions in the United States. It cannot attract the numbers it requires from among native-born Americans, who, faced with many attractive alternatives, are less inclined to enter the service of the Church. And for most of our recent history, the tensions in politics have not been such as to attract and hold a large number whose lives are dedicated to public service. But in every generation some have been willing to devote their lives to causes: to missionary work among the heathen; to the improvement of the handicapped at home; to the eradication of racial conflict; to the organization of workers; to the elimination of war; to radical reform of society; to the propagation of a new religion or the strengthening of an established one.

The types of work pursued by those who belong to the ideological type indicate that these individuals differ from the run of mankind. They are likely to be much more complex people who are able to set themselves off from the rest of the community in the goals that they seek, in the efforts they make, and in the risks that they are willing to run. An extreme example is the martyr.

But not all who have ideological commitments, even deep commitments, can or must work them out in their occupational lives. In our society jobs have come to take only a part of a man's energies, and many with strong commitments can find opportunities for realizing them in other sectors of their lives. As we know, a great many do just that. We need refer only to the lay leaders of many social welfare organizations and the activists in political parties. In fact, there can be congruence or conflict between a man's working life and his life off the job. For example, a captain of industry who is interested in better race relations and who devotes much of his free time to this end has an opportunity to live by his commitments in his business by helping to open opportunities to those who have been discriminated against. But a staff specialist who is a Negro and devotes most of his time off the job to race relations may find himself in a working environment where he must tolerate negative attitudes and prejudice on the part of his associates which inhibit him from pressing the social goals which mean so much to him.

We see then that the four types that we have developed in connection with our study of educated men pursuing professional or scientific careers do have applicability to a much broader band of people. We limited ourselves to four types, among other reasons to avoid undue complications in the analysis. However, a study which is focused on a more diversified group might have to introduce several additional types to capture adequately the variability in value orientations that exist towards work in our society.

The classification of people in terms of a dominant value orientation towards their work, however much it may be rationalized, did result in severe constrictions. For this reason we will introduce here two additional conceptions that will enable us to broaden and deepen the analysis. The first relates to the distinction between the work and nonwork areas of life. Increasingly, people are able to seek and find satisfactions not only through their jobs but also through the purposeful activities that they engage in off their jobs. The second point has to do with the relationship between the two: people can follow one of three patterns which relate their activities off the job to their career concerns. Their nonwork activities can reinforce, complement, or compensate for their activities at work.

This larger framework makes it possible to take account of a wider play of values and more diversified behavior. A lawyer who misses the opportunity to play a leadership role in his work may become active in community affairs. He can thus realize a value which is important to him—leadership—in his nonwork activities. Or a businessman who has not been as successful as he had hoped may throw himself into church and social welfare activities from which he derives some compensation for the disappointments in his work.

Table 16 presents the distribution of our group among the four value types.

That half of our group were classified as the individualistic type is noteworthy but not too surprising in light of its special characteristics. These men had made a substantial

TABLE 16. *Value orientation, in percent*

| Value Orientation Percent | Percent |
| --- | --- |
| Individualistic | 50 |
| Leadership | 18 |
| Social | 27 |
| Ideological | 5 |
| Total | 100 |

investment of time and effort in finding the type of work they preferred. They wanted to be masters of themselves, and they wanted to dictate their own patterns of working. It is this orientation that may explain at least in part why they were willing to make such a big investment in preparing for work.

In view of the outstanding ability of the respondents, the relatively small number who were classified as the leadership type might at first appear surprising, since we could expect those with superior ability to seek and gain power. The small proportion who fall into this category may reflect the fact that the key sector of contemporary life in which men can find an outlet for leadership proclivities is in corporate enterprise. But people heading for top positions in business do not have to pursue graduate or professional education; this was surely so in the early postwar years. Therefore our selection produced a group with a smaller number of individuals with leadership orientation than might be found in another group with superior ability.

The proportion of social types can at one and the same

time be considered large and small. It is relatively large in view of the long period of preparation for work undertaken by our group. We might have thought that such people would be more strongly directed to find work in which they would be masters of their own destiny, and to be less concerned about relationships with superiors and colleagues. On the other hand the proportion is relatively small considering the emphasis placed on social adjustment in our society.

We might have expected that only a small percent would be characterized as the ideological type since those with this kind of value commitment are unlikely to pursue their education beyond college.

Before concluding this analysis of value orientations, let us see in what manner this axis is related, if at all, to the two earlier axes which dealt with career patterns and levels of achievement. Table 17 sets forth the relationships between the value types and career patterns.

TABLE 17. *Career pattern and value orientation, in percent* (N = 279)

|  | Value Orientation | | | |
|---|---|---|---|---|
|  | *individualistic* | *leadership* | *social* | *ideological* |
| Career pattern |  |  |  |  |
| Straight | 67 | 56 | 49 | 53 |
| Broad | 22 | 34 | 33 | 27 |
| Variant | 11 | 10 | 18 | 20 |
| Total | 100 | 100 | 100 | 100 |

The first point to note is that the relationships are somewhat tenuous. Nevertheless, a few formulations may be ventured. Compared to the leadership and social types, a relatively higher proportion of the individualistic type is found in the straight pattern and a relatively smaller proportion in the broad pattern. This probably reflects the tendency of those who place a premium on autonomy in their work to remain in the same field if their first job meets this dominant need.

The finding that the leadership type was rather prominently represented in the broad pattern may reflect the process of accumulating power in our society which usually forces a man to branch out beyond his original field of activity. The relatively higher proportion of the social type in the variant pattern may reflect their inability to move as directly as many in the straight pattern from an interest in an area to a field or function. Perhaps the goal they were seeking in their work was elusive because they did not know quite what they were seeking. Hence they were more likely to experience delays and changes in getting into an occupational groove.

The very small numbers who comprise the ideological type make even a tentative formulation questionable. There is, however, a suggestion that a higher than average proportion of this type may also be engaged in a prolonged and uncertain search before they find their occupational objectives.

The other major relationship to explore is that between the value types and achievement levels. These are set out in Table 18.

TABLE 18. *Achievement level and value orientation, in percent* (N = 279)

| | Value Orientation | | | |
| --- | --- | --- | --- | --- |
| | individualistic | leadership | social | ideological |
| Achievement level | | | | |
| Upper | 32 | 36 | 28 | 33 |
| Intermediate | 38 | 44 | 29 | 27 |
| Lower | 30 | 20 | 43 | 40 |
| Total | 100 | 100 | 100 | 100 |

There was no reason to expect a pronounced concentration of the individualistic type in any achievement level and that is what in fact the table revealed. And we might have anticipated the tendency of the leadership type to land in the higher achievement levels, perhaps even more than in fact occurred. Since we have learned of the delays that many in the social type experienced in getting started on their careers, a drift towards the lower achievement level for this group was to have been expected.

The most important aspect of the relationships presented in the last two tables is the support which they offer our hypothesis that value orientations are key elements in occupational development and deserve to rank with career patterns and achievement levels as a major analytical axis.

# 8

# Work Satisfactions

Everything that we have learned so far about the career development of our group—their preparation for work, their employment history, their level of achievement, and their basic value orientations—attests to their search for the type of work which will yield them a high degree of satisfaction. Their desire for achieving fulfillment and gratification in work helps explain their heavy investment in preparation. Their intellectual abilities and their superior education gave them a range of options far beyond that available to most members of the labor force. There is an element of unreality to many investigations of the work satisfactions of employees who have limited skills and therefore limited job options. And there are surprisingly few investigations of work satisfaction among the talented. The highly developed skills and multiple options found in our group heightens the significance of their adjustment to work.

A first approach to the study of work satisfactions might be to consider the statements that individuals make about their work, favorable and unfavorable. We can begin but cannot end there. If a man says, "I'm tired of being a professor," we know that he is dissatisfied with that occupational activity. But his statement alone does not tell us

which of the functions he performs as a professor are
frustrating to him, or whether this is merely an offhand
remark made at the end of a hectic semester or whether it
actually reflects a disenchantment with his career.

Isolated statements about what one likes or does not like
about work cannot be used directly to assess work satisfaction or dissatisfaction. This can be done only if specific
statements about work can be related to other aspects of
personality, particularly to values and goals. A review of the
range of statements that people make about their work and
specifically whether they find it satisfactory reveals that
they seldom if ever consider their work in its entirety.
Rather they single out for favorable or unfavorable comment one or another facet of the whole. They frequently
make both positive and negative statements about the same
job. Consider the industrial chemist who is happy with his
salary and his co-workers but who bemoans his lack of
opportunity to do basic research; the government official
who knows that he is engaged in work of high social significance but who frets about the cumbersome bureaucratic
machinery within which he must operate; the professor who
loves to teach but who finds it almost distasteful to mark
papers.

In our earlier study of *Occupational Choice* we distinguished three types of people in terms of the fulcrum of
their search for work satisfaction: those who seek primarily
intrinsic satisfactions; those who are concerned with the
rewards from work—above all, income; and those who seek
concomitant satisfactions, such as agreeable companions and
a pleasant working environment.

In the present study we asked the respondents to single
out the most gratifying and the least gratifying aspects of
their work, and on the basic of their replies we developed a

category scheme of these aspects. We divided them into five major divisions: nature of work, self-expression, freedom, social contribution, and rewards and concomitants. The following quotations provide an initial indication of what the respondents wrote about the most gratifying aspects of their work.

A history professor commented, "I get paid for doing exactly what I want to do—read and study, teach, and help others do the same." A social researcher enjoys most "the opportunity to observe and describe the ways people work together." These are examples of those who were gratified by the nature of their work.

Sometimes a respondent listed particular aspects of his career that gave him greatest satisfaction, such as the physician who disliked basic research but cited as gratifying "the care of patients and the teaching of medical students, interns, and residents in medicine," and the mathematics professor who preferred "working with some of the more gifted students in more advanced courses." Others mentioned the diversity of their work; a professor of geology wrote of "the freedom from boredom and detail and routine."

As an example of self-expression as a satisfying aspect, a philosophy professor wrote about "a sense of growth in the discovery of new ideas and perspectives and reexamination of old ideas in new light." Self-expression can also involve interaction with others such as "the transfer of an informed, vitalizing experience of my own learning to something similar in students" noted by a philosophy professor; or a U.S. public affairs officer's reference to "contact with foreigners and the occasional evidence that I have influenced their thinking."

The category "freedom" means, not free time, but independence of action. A newspaper editor is most gratified by "freedom to call editorial shots as I see them." An English and Latin professor is most satisfied by "the fact that I can to some extent lead Aristotle's 'Life of Contemplation' and get paid for it."

The director of development engineering of a major electronics concern mentioned the satisfactions which he receives from the social contribution of his work: "Work to be done makes significant contribution to society on an international front and exercises a wide range of my talents and interests." A similar aspect was commented on by an educational missionary who found pleasure in the "knowledge that the primary school system I administered is able to run now with 100 percent African administration and teaching."

The element of status, which belongs to the category of rewards and concomitants, is important in the following comment of a Far Eastern expert: "The feeling of satisfaction that I am considered to be a leading man in my field both here and Japan." Another concomitant, pleasure in the conditions of work, was noted by a professor of history who enjoyed the "opportunity to meet a variety of persons outside academic life and to travel in connection with conferences, etc.," while a chemical company executive enjoyed interpersonal relations with "capable, intelligent workers and associates." Satisfaction with income was mentioned by the patent expert who reported "a salary somewhat higher than the average for same years of service in the same company."

Equally indicative of the complex nature of work satisfactions was the wide range of statements made by the respondents about the least gratifying aspects of their work.

There were some who singled out as least gratifying the nature of their work, such as the European representative of a large chemical company who bemoaned his "removal from active research" and the intelligence expert in the State Department who regretted "absence from full-time teaching."

Many cited particular aspects of their work, such as the professor of sociology who called attention to "the onerous burden of committee work, faculty meetings, staff meetings, and administrative procedure," or, as a chemistry professor described them, "the duties which are not of a creative type but only 'make-work.'" A law professor was unhappy about "exam grading and other prosaica of academic life." A museum curator objected to "answering stupid questions of the ignorant public."

Lack of stimulation was a cause of dissatisfaction. A vice-president of a consulting firm mentioned "the need to accept certain contracts for relatively routine types of work in order to maintain and expand the volume of company business," and a research chemist specified "the occasional tedious portions of a research program." Much the same complaint was made by a professor of geology who was dissatisfied with "routine teaching of basic skills and techniques."

Impediments to self-expression were singled out by some of the respondents. An individual research scientist scored "the frustrations of the work and even more the dissipation of energy in fruitless projects one is pressed into doing." A professor of philosophy bemoaned the fact that "there are too many books unread, colleagues with their own problems don't apparently see mine, the article is not published, etc. In short, failure of some kind." A mathematics professor used these words to describe his discontent: "Slowness of application of advances I have made."

Others were disturbed by a lack of responsiveness: "Occasionally I have been faced with poor students and the feeling that their doltish expressions will confront me for an entire year is certainly disheartening." A research chemist wrote about the "failure of appreciation by management of certain aspects of an investigation." An American consul commented on the "general lack of appreciation of interest by public in work."

Certain respondents felt hampered. An associate economist of a leading bank remarked on the "lack of time and freedom to seriously consider issues before adopting policy standpoints." An instrumentation specialist called attention to the "administrative structures which tend to interfere with main interests."

Some found it disturbing if their work had little social significance. A professor of physics was dissatisfied because of "a general feeling that the study and teaching of physics is of very little use in view of man's tremendous physical, social, and spiritual needs."

Many of the group, although they were not primarily concerned with achieving a high income or positions of power and status, were dissatisfied with the income which they earned and the concomitant rewards. A considerable number were disturbed by the fact that they were earning less than they thought they were worth or less than they needed to support a family. A computer researcher reported as an unsatisfying aspect of work the "relatively low salaries of scientists compared to less valuable and sometimes harmful 'workers,' such as many in 'administration' or 'public relations.'" An English professor was dissatisfied with "a salary that is low contrasted to that of friends of comparable age, education, and achievement in other fields." And a chemistry professor plaintively remarked on the fact that "our recent Ph.D. graduates frequently make more on their first job than I do after seven years."

Others were dissatisfied with their status. A senior staff specialist in an industrial organization called attention to "the anonymity of major research and publications failing to give outside credit where credit is due"; a government research chemist: "No status—although I am on the senior staff, my responsibilities (true of 90 percent of the senior staff) are limited to my research."

Some complained about such concomitants as the location of their work or its scheduling. A newspaper writer: "The hours . . . evening work twice a week." A professor of economics in the Midwest: "Having to live in what to me is a small town." A novelist: "It is lonely, grueling work." A professor of history in the South: "—— is situated in a climate of local opinion that is anti-intellectual and often hostile to independent thought. Within the university, however, there is full academic freedom and congeniality."

Poor interpersonal relations were another source of discontent. A staff specialist in a large petroleum organization mentioned the "competition of persons who are interested only in title and in protecting themselves against criticism." The technical director of an industrial laboratory found difficulty in "dealing with sales oriented management superiors." An economics professor wrote of "the lack of intellectual stimulation from my colleagues, partly because so many of them are third-rate, partly because the atmosphere of the institution does not encourage the interchange of ideas." And a philosophy professor was unhappy about "the petty political infighting so common to academic departments; dependence on administrative favor."

And finally, there were those who were disturbed by the general conditions affecting either their particular jobs or their chosen careers. For example, a professor of French spoke of "the largely uncompetitive, professionally limited nature of academic work. This is the only profession I know of in the United States where a person with superior talents, and willing to exert himself to the utmost, would, after twenty or thirty years engaged in a career, come out *only slightly better* than someone of very mediocre ability who would do only the minimum work expected of him." A professor of economics: "Pressures to publish for the sake of getting one's name in print, rather than as really worthwhile research. A bias against rewards on the basis of teaching ability and a broad range of interests." And a laboratory director: "Personnel problems, low salaries, incompetent help, a frequent and rapid turnover which prevents training personnel to assume some of my responsibilities."

Our respondents found more to praise than to complain about in their work. From the group as a whole there were approximately four positive responses to every three negative comments.

The three major categories that refer to intrinsic work satisfactions, that is, satisfactions which are inherent in the work that people perform (nature of work, self-expression, and freedom) account for almost three-quarters of all positive responses. In contrast, only 1 in 5 of the responses singled out the specifically extrinsic satisfactions such as income, status, conditions of work, and social relations as a principal source of work satisfaction, as indicated in Table 19.

The relatively low percentage of responses that singled

TABLE 19. *Most and least gratifying aspects of work, in percent of responses* (N = 268)

| Aspects | most gratifying (R = 403) | | least gratifying (R = 299) | |
|---|---|---|---|---|
| Nature of work | 28 | | 49 | |
| basic interests | | 16 | | 2 |
| particular activities | | 9 | | 30 |
| stimulation | | 3 | | 17 |
| Self-expression | 36 | | 10 | |
| self-realization | | 24 | | 6 |
| responsiveness of others | | 12 | | 4 |
| Freedom | 9 | | 2 | |
| Social contribution | 8 | | 1 | |
| Rewards and concomitants | 20 | | 38 | |
| income | | 3 | | 7 |
| status | | 4 | | 3 |
| conditions of work | | 4 | | 20 |
| social relations | | 9 | | 8 |
| Total | 100 | | 100 | |

out "freedom" as a source of special gratification probably reflects the fact that many members of our group took it for granted. Had we asked them to identify which of a number of jobs they would not consider acceptable, many would probably have selected those in which their freedom would be limited.

Several observations are suggested by the responses about the negative aspects of work. Only a very few comments indicated that the individual's basic interests were not met by his work. But a high proportion singled out particular aspects as burdensome or unrewarding. While many felt that the rewards were insufficient, they were more concerned about the concomitants, such as the environment, than about income and status. The detailed comments reveal that the respondents complained most about the absence of stimulating social or cultural contacts in their working environment. This type of deprivation is closely akin to dissatisfaction with certain intrinsic aspects of work.

We can now take the next step and explore whether the satisfactions that people derive from their work are connected with the fields which they have chosen, the function which they perform, and the employer for whom they work. Table 20 presents the data with respect to fields of work.

With the exception of those in the social sciences the largest group of respondents in each field singled out self-expression as the most gratifying aspect of their work. And with the exception of those in engineering, all of the others selected the nature of their work as the second source of satisfaction.

An inspection of more detailed data provided some interesting sidelights. Those in the humanities who were most gratified by the rewards and concomitants of their work situation were not interested in income and status or even in working conditions; it was the interpersonal relations which they found particularly satisfying. The social scientists were most satisfied with the particular activities of their work.

Table 21 presents the most gratifying aspects of work according to the respondents' function.

Inspection of the data grouped by type of function which the respondents performed indicates that each group found one of the principal sources of their satisfaction to be self-expression. With regard to the second source of satisfaction, the most striking finding is the high proportion of those in a professional capacity who singled out rewards and concomitants. The relatively high proportion of those in research who selected freedom and those in staff functions

TABLE 20. *Most gratifying aspects of work and occupational field, in percent of responses* (R = 403)

| Gratifying aspects | Occupational Field | | | | |
|---|---|---|---|---|---|
| | *humanities* | *social sciences* | *natural sciences* | *engineering* | *business and professional* |
| Nature of work | 27 | 35 | 26 | 7 | 31 |
| Self-expression | 38 | 27 | 38 | 56 | 38 |
| Freedom | 6 | 9 | 14 | 10 | 5 |
| Social contribution | 6 | 8 | 6 | 17 | 5 |
| Rewards and concomitants | 23 | 21 | 16 | 10 | 21 |
| Total | 100 | 100 | 100 | 100 | 100 |

TABLE 21. *Most gratifying aspects of work and type of work, in percent of responses* (R = 403)

| | | | | Type of Work | | | |
|---|---|---|---|---|---|---|---|
| Gratifying aspects | teaching | teaching and research | research | research and administration | administration | staff | professional |
| Nature of work | 32 | 39 | 13 | 15 | 15 | 26 | 21 |
| Self-expression | 30 | 31 | 38 | 52 | 52 | 36 | 29 |
| Freedom | 10 | 9 | 21 | 15 | 6 | 2 | 0 |
| Social contribution | 7 | 3 | 5 | 11 | 10 | 18 | 0 |
| Rewards and concomitants | 21 | 18 | 23 | 7 | 17 | 18 | 50 |
| Total | 100 | 100 | 100 | 100 | 100 | 100 | 100 |

who mentioned the social contribution of their work should also be noted.

The third set of data relate the gratifying aspects of work to the institutional setting in which the respondents are employed; see Table 22.

TABLE 22. *Most gratifying aspects of work and institutional setting, in percent of responses* (R = 403)

*Institutional Setting*

| | academic | corporate | non-profit | government | self-employed |
|---|---|---|---|---|---|
| Gratifying aspects | | | | | |
| Nature of work | 34 | 23 | 13 | 17 | 12 |
| Self-expression | 33 | 44 | 37 | 38 | 35 |
| Freedom | 9 | 6 | 21 | 6 | 6 |
| Social contribution | 5 | 8 | 11 | 33 | 0 |
| Rewards and concomitants | 19 | 19 | 18 | 6 | 47 |
| Total | 100 | 100 | 100 | 100 | 100 |

The data grouped according to institutional setting in which the respondents worked indicate that each group identified self-expression as one of the two major sources of work satisfaction. With respect to the second principal source of satisfaction, those in academic life and in corporate enterprise selected the nature of their work; those in nonprofit institutions, freedom; those in government, social contribution; the self-employed, rewards and concomitants.

Despite the homogeneity of our group, at least in terms of their prolonged preparation for work, there was a considerable variability among those in the same field, function, or institutional setting as to the most gratifying element of their work. We see then that work satisfaction is a complex and subtle phenomenon which cannot be fully captured even by such elaborate category schemes as we have employed.

There remains one additional analysis that may contribute to the further illumination of the complex nature of work satisfaction. An analysis of the respondents' statements about work satisfactions and dissatisfactions in terms of our three axial categories—career patterns, achievement levels, and value orientations—may yield some additional information.

TABLE 23. *Most gratifying aspects of work and career pattern, in percent of responses* (R = 403)

|  | Career Pattern | | |
|---|---|---|---|
|  | *straight* | *broad* | *variant* |
| Gratifying aspects |  |  |  |
| Nature of work | 29 | 27 | 23 |
| Self-expression | 36 | 36 | 36 |
| Freedom | 9 | 12 | 4 |
| Social contribution | 7 | 9 | 6 |
| Rewards and concomitants | 19 | 16 | 31 |
| Total | 100 | 100 | 100 |

Table 23 reveals no significant differences among those in the three career patterns with regard to the source of their work satisfactions other than the relatively greater satisfaction that those in the variant pattern ascribed to rewards and concomitants in general; this refers here to their relations with their co-workers rather than to income and status.

We might assume that in a competitive society the relations between an individual's achievement level and his work satisfaction would be sharper than between his career pattern and his work satisfaction. Table 24 presents the satisfying aspects of work in relation to achievement level.

TABLE 24. *Most gratifying aspects of work and achievement level, in percent of responses* (R = 403)

| | Achievement Level | | |
| --- | --- | --- | --- |
| | upper | intermediate | lower |
| Gratifying aspects | | | |
| Nature of work | 30 | 24 | 29 |
| Self-expression | 37 | 40 | 31 |
| Freedom | 6 | 14 | 8 |
| Social contribution | 7 | 10 | 6 |
| Rewards and concomitants | 20 | 12 | 26 |
| Total | 100 | 100 | 100 |

Once again the findings are not particularly significant. The relatively high proportion of those in the lower achievement level who found their major satisfactions in rewards and concomitants might seem surprising until we learn that they single out as particularly gratifying, not income and status, but their social relations at work. The relatively high percentage of those in the top achievement level who are dissatisfied with the nature of their work may reflect nothing more than the dissatisfaction of those who have done well in their chosen field but do not see where they can go from here. In general, the striking finding is the relatively modest differences in the types of work satisfaction between those in the top and bottom achievement levels.

One final relationship remains to be probed, that between the types of value orientations which people hold toward work and their work satisfactions. Table 25 presents these data.

Respondents in each type reported as the two primary sources of their satisfaction self-expression and the nature of

TABLE 25. *Most gratifying aspects of work and value orientation, in percent of responses* (R = 403)

| | Value Orientation | | | |
|---|---|---|---|---|
| | *individualistic* | *leadership* | *social* | *ideological* |
| Gratifying aspects | | | | |
| Nature of work | 35 | 25 | 22 | 25 |
| Self-expression | 33 | 37 | 38 | 33 |
| Freedom | 14 | 7 | 8 | 0 |
| Social contribution | 5 | 9 | 9 | 25 |
| Rewards and concomitants | 13 | 22 | 23 | 17 |
| Total | 100 | 100 | 100 | 100 |

work. The proportion of those in the leadership and social types who selected rewards and concomitants as a source of satisfaction was however greater than among the individualistic type.

The complexity of work satisfactions precludes any simple summary. Yet several findings can be distilled from the foregoing analysis, and a few additional inferences may be ventured. There are many different facets of work that may be the principal source of an individual's satisfactions or dissatisfactions; in fact the same broad area may be the principal source of both his satisfactions and dissatisfactions.

The fields of work, the functions which people perform at work, and the institutional settings in which they work were found to be significantly related to the satisfactions they derive from their work. On the other hand, neither the type of career pattern which they follow nor their achievement level was closely related to the satisfying or unsatisfying aspects of their work. But significant relationships were found between the type of value orientations that people hold towards their work and the sources of their satisfactions and dissatisfactions.

So much for findings. What about the inferences? Again it is important to stress that our group was composed of people who underwent a very long period of preparation presumably because they placed a high value on securing the type of work and career which they would find satisfying. Hence working in a field of their choice, performing the type of functions which they preferred, and finding a congenial employment situation were matters of moment to the members of our group. Their search for work satisfaction was more intense than for other people.

The fact that they were intellectuals also helps to explain why they placed such importance on the satisfactions which they were able to derive from the more intrinsic aspects of work. It is not that they were indifferent to such matters as income and status, but that they valued other aspects more, particularly the nature of work, and the opportunity for self-expression.

One final point. Our group, which was concerned about work satisfaction, was in an excellent position to achieve it. They came to the labor market exceptionally well prepared; they started their careers at a time when the economy was characterized by a strong demand for well-trained people; and this strong demand persisted throughout the period during which they were getting established. They had many options, and the environment offered them excellent opportunities to pursue them. Here was a group of men who came to know what they wanted from work and who were in a good position to find what they wanted.

# 9

# Self-Realization

The last chapter left a major question unresolved. We found a relatively good fit between the respondents and their work. Did this mean that they had come to like what they were doing? Or did it mean that they were doing the kind of work they had always wanted to do and had set out to do? Or were both of these factors operating to bring about the high level of work satisfaction that was found to prevail?

Our early chapters offer evidence on these alternative explanations. We found that most of the members of our group had determined on their occupational choice in their late teens when they were in college, and that the choice which they had then crystallized and later specified had provided a direction for their subsequent career decisions. It is therefore unlikely that the first hypothesis suggested above, that they had come to like their work, is correct. They did not fall into their careers; they had selected them. The second hypothesis, that they were content with the type of work they had selected, is more acceptable. It suggests that the satisfactions which these men derive from their work are primarily the result of their being in the fortunate position of realizing many, if not all, of their career objectives.

This chapter will consider the relations between expectations and performance, as one approach to understanding the satisfactions a man seeks not only from work but from all his areas of endeavor. Our analysis will be structured around the way an individual reaches decisions about alternative career choices and employment opportunities so that he can move one or two steps closer to his goals. His decisions transcend his concern about the present. More often than not he introduces into his calculations long-range considerations, considerations that appear to be guided by a projection of what he wants to be, or become, in the future. He engages in what might be described as a process of *self-realization*.

The career patterns analyzed earlier are suggestive of this process of self-realization; they indicate that the successive stages of the career development of our group are not random, but reflect order and direction. However, such order and direction might attest solely to the force of external determinants: people have been compelled to follow certain lines of work because of the circumstances of the labor market.

An alternative hypothesis to explain the regularities in the career patterns is that one's career is a function of training. For example, long and specialized education is a major determinant of later career development. If a man pursues specialized studies, especially if he earns a doctorate, his career is likely to be set in the field in which he trains.

Although either external considerations, such as existing market conditions, or prior education and training may prove determining, the career development of our group cannot be adequately explained without taking account of an important internal factor. Most of our group gave repeated evidence of a desire to relate their present circumstances to a future goal. In responding to job offers they assessed more than such directly relevant criteria as income, rank, and working conditions. They also weighed the alternatives against some future goals. Many sensed that certain offers might bring them closer to where they wanted to be in the future and therefore should be accepted; but often an offer, attractive on its own terms, was rejected because the respondent felt that it would interfere with a long-range objective. Sometimes an offer was accepted as a "holding operation" even though it held little promise of bringing the individual closer to his long range goal.

For some, career interruption is simply a delay; others may be deflected and never get back on their original track; still others succeed in building on an interruption so that they may even accelerate their progress towards their original goal or toward a goal that they have modified as a result of unexpected occurrences. Most of our group experienced a career interruption as a result of World War II. The decisions that they made subsequent to that interruption reflect whether and to what extent their objectives and goals exercised a controlling influence over their decision-making. Sometimes an interruption early in one's life can contribute to the clarification of his goals. Several of our respondents indicated that during their military service they had been able to clarify their occupational perspectives.

Another indication of the manner in which the individual's orientation to the future plays a prominent role in his occupational determination was found in the decisions made by those who followed broad career patterns. In this spectrum are the individuals who shifted their field of work or the functions which they were performing. But when their moves are traced we find that they were not random;

they were tied meaningfully not only to their previous field or activity but also in a shrouded manner to a new goal that likewise is related to an earlier objective.

The most persuasive evidence of the importance of the orientation towards the future in the shaping of a career is found in the variant pattern. Included in the variant pattern were some who were floundering because they did not have a clear image of what they wanted to be in the future. Others had to abandon the career objective which they had determined upon because of the variance between their goal and the intervening reality which they encountered. And still others were caught up in a very long process of seeking to realize a difficult goal, such as the composer or novelist who wanted to produce a first-rate piece of work.

Further evidence of the way in which career development is embedded in a time-transcending process is found in the value orientation towards work that characterized the members of our group. Differences in value orientation were grounded in differences in the goals and objectives which the members hoped to achieve through work. These differences were found to be deeply rooted and more or less fixed.

Although the data concerned with work satisfaction were centered primarily around the individual's current work, they contained an element of futurity. We found, for instance, that there were significant relationships between the value orientations of people towards their work and the type of work satisfactions which they sought. But here, as in the other cited instances, the role of the future was incidental rather than central to the analysis.

There are substantial differences in the way individuals handle the role of the future in their career development.

Some early have finely etched pictures of what they want to become, others have only a hazy notion, still others fall in between. But with the passage of time the future is transformed into the present; as this occurs, the individual measures his present circumstances against his earlier expectations. As he progresses through life his expectations usually do not remain fixed but undergo varying degrees of transformation, affected by the congruence and the discrepancies between the goals that he has set for himself and his realization of them. There is a dynamism to this process of self-realization; the key is in the degree of congruence that the individual achieves or fails to achieve between his expectations and his actual life experiences.

We based our study of the process of self-realization on three distinct but related bodies of information. The first has a retrospective orientation: we sought to elicit from the respondents the extent to which they felt that their earlier expectations had been met. Next, we sought information about the respondents' anticipations about their future career development. Finally, we sought to understand the underlying determinants of their expectations by analyzing their answers to a series of hypothetical questions about the way in which they might respond to future alternatives affecting their work and careers.

A simple category scheme can contribute a great deal to illuminating the counterpoint between expectations and reality. The expectations that a person has may be exceeded by what he is able to accomplish in the future. Or there may be a rough equivalency between what he looks forward to accomplishing and what he in fact is able to accomplish. In that instance one can say that his expectations were met. Or he may fail to accomplish what he expected to achieve.

In this instance his expectations are unfulfilled. Finally, since expectations are always multiple, it is possible that some will be exceeded or met while others are unfulfilled.

Once again, we ordered the replies of our respondents in terms of their comments about the nature of work, self-expression, freedom, social contribution, and rewards and concomitants. The first three are concerned with the intrinsic aspects of work, the last two with the extrinsic aspects. The following quotations, ordered according to the foregoing schema, indicate how the respondents described their expectations about various aspects of their work and career and the extent to which they were or were not met.

With respect to the intrinsic aspects, a professor of law remarked, "My direct contacts with students, both as a counselor and a teacher, are even more rewarding than I anticipated." A program analyst said, "The type of 'intellectual puzzle-solving' . . . is so interesting to me that it is not really work." A professor of chemistry commented that, "The research work of my group has worked out better than I originally hoped." The counsel of a large trade association reported that he "had not foreseen that *real* business problems can be fully as complex, challenging, interesting as the more hypothetical or historical academic issues."

With respect to the specific aspect of freedom in work, a tax economist working for a large public utility reported his "greater than expected freedom of movement and thought—limited but still exceeding expectations." A successful chemical manufacturer was pleased to find that "self-employment allows great success." And a philosophy professor found that he had "greater independence in the development of courses" than he had originally anticipated.

The foregoing comments suggest that some of our respondents were pleasantly surprised to find that they received greater intrinsic satisfactions from their work than they had anticipated. Many, however, were disappointed.

An English professor wrote, "I had hoped by now to get rid of freshman teaching, which while not unrewarding involves considerable drudgery. As it is, I am teaching at every level of the organization—freshman, sophomore, junior, senior, and graduate. I feel scattered." An industrial research scientist resented that "requests of the organization are pressing me into areas of development somewhat remote from greatest interest and strength." An associate director of an industrial research laboratory called attention to "the amount of time that I must spend on 'business' rather than 'science' and the resulting shallowness of my own understanding of science even in my own field." Complaints about lack of time for their own work were also made by academicians. A professor of organic chemistry complained of "less time (and energy) for personal growth," and a department chairman in another university said, "I have too little time to devote to research."

So far the comments have been focused on expectations involving the intrinsic aspects of work. The following excerpts deal with the external aspects, particularly such matters as income, status, and other conditions in the working environment. A professor of economics was pleasantly surprised about his income: "Salary above expectations when I entered field." Another academician, an associate professor of music, wrote, "Considering the many financial problems of a music career, I think I have been fortunate indeed." A more subtle point was made by an aerospace scientist in industry, who replied: "I had not expected so large a salary, thinking in terms of 1940 dollars, not pinching pennies."

Many were pleasantly surprised by the status which they had been able to achieve. A law professor wrote that his "position and prestige in the community is greater than I had expected." A public relations expert commented, "My growing professional status as a political public relations advisor is a surprise." A professor of French at a large Midwestern university said that "the only aspect of my career that has exceeded my expectations is the relative ease with which I had advanced in academic status."

Some were surprised by the conditions of their work which were better than expected. A professor of history commented: "More opportunity for foreign travel, part-time work in the government than I had anticipated." Another academic, a professor of English, had not anticipated the "cheerful and beneficial association of colleagues."

Once again, however, others were disappointed with the external circumstances which they encountered. A marketing executive for a small steel company said bluntly that he was disappointed with his "salary and income." An industrial research chemist with a major oil company also felt that his "remuneration could be greater." A college professor of geology reported a mixed conclusion: "The financial rewards are most disappointing; the intangibles and my satisfaction in my work are all that could be desired."

Some respondents felt that they had not acquired sufficient status. A journalist wrote, "Certainly my career has been delayed in its financial progress by so much moving . . . But the sowing of wild oats has brought about only a marking in time—until now." A trial lawyer also blamed a late start: "Have not achieved professional stature which should have been achieved by now owing in part to late start in private practice." The head of a hospital department of chemistry wrote, "I had desired to distinguish myself more in the field of basic bio-chemical research." A recently promoted assistant professor of geology noted, "I only recently received my appointment to assist. prof. which I think was long over due. I now have to 'catch up.' "

Some of the group found themselves working under conditions that were less favorable than they had anticipated. A law professor complained about "too many demands on my time for functions having little or nothing to do with teaching and research and which surely interfere with them." An industrial economist reported "the difficulty of achieving my desire for pure research with the necessity of focusing on corporate goal."

Despite the wide range of replies about their expectations concerning the intrinsic and external aspects of their work and the extent to which they had or had not been met, we did not encounter any special difficulty in ordering them within the following simple schema. Table 26 is based on replies from 97 percent of the 279 respondents who filled in the detailed questionnaires.

TABLE 26. *Fulfillment of expectations, in percent* $(N = 272)$

|  | *Percent* |
|---|---|
| Fulfillment | |
| Expectations exceeded | 18 |
| Expectations met | 49 |
| Some expectations met; some not met | 16 |
| Expectations not met | 17 |
| Total | 100 |

From this we see that two-thirds of the entire group reported that all of their expectations had been met or exceeded. The remaining third is about equally divided

between those who reported that some of their expectations
had been met while others had not, and those who reported
that their expectations had not been fulfilled. Thus only
about 1 in 7 submitted a completely negative report.

More detailed data indicate which facets of their career
exceeded and which did not meet their expectations. The
most striking finding is that it was the internal aspects of
their work which most frequently exceeded their expectations, and the external considerations which most frequently
fell short. Income and status were not singled out with conspicuous frequency either by those who reported that their
expectations had been exceeded or those whose expectations
were unmet. It may well be that the members of a group
that is so heavily concentrated in academic work and research early had a fairly realistic view of these external
considerations and further that these facets of a career were
not of overwhelming concern to them.

We can now relate the data about expectations to the
three analytical axes. Table 27 presents the relationship between expectations and career patterns.

TABLE 27. *Expectations and career patterns, in percent* (N = 272)

|  | Career Pattern | | |
| --- | --- | --- | --- |
|  | *straight* | *broad* | *variant* |
| Fulfillment |  |  |  |
| Expectations exceeded | 16 | 27 | 14 |
| Expectations met | 52 | 41 | 45 |
| Some expectations met; some not met | 16 | 15 | 19 |
| Expectations not met | 16 | 17 | 22 |
| Total | 100 | 100 | 100 |

No strongly significant relationships are revealed although
those respondents who followed a broad pattern were more
likely to feel that their expectations had been exceeded.

Table 28 sets forth the relationships between expectations and achievement level.

TABLE 28. *Expectations and achievement level, in percent* (N = 272)

| Fulfillment | Achievement Level | | |
|---|---|---|---|
| | upper | intermediate | lower |
| Expectations exceeded | 26 | 15 | 13 |
| Expectations met | 53 | 51 | 42 |
| Some expectations met; some not met | 11 | 11 | 28 |
| Expectations not met | 10 | 23 | 17 |
| Total | 100 | 100 | 100 |

Several significant findings emerge from this comparison. The largest proportion in each achievement level reported that their expectations had been met. Those in the upper level were much more likely to report that their expectations had been exceeded. As one would expect, a relatively high proportion of those in the lower achievement level said that their expectations had not been met or had been met only in part. More striking is the relatively high proportion in the intermediate level who reported that their expectations had not been met. This may reflect that this group had higher goals or that for some reason they encountered difficulty in realizing their goals.

The third axial approach, given in Table 29, relates value orientations towards work to fulfillment of expectations.

A consideration of the three major types—the ideological contained a relatively small number—indicates that those in the leadership category were much more likely than the others to report that their expectations had been exceeded. Nothing else of significance emerges from the table.

The relatively small number of significant relationships

TABLE 29. *Expectations and value orientation, in percent* (N = 272)

| Fulfillment | individualistic | leadership | social | ideological |
|---|---|---|---|---|
| | *Value Orientation* | | | |
| Expectations exceeded | 19 | 29 | 9 | 29 |
| Expectations met | 48 | 40 | 55 | 42 |
| Some expectations met; some not met | 14 | 21 | 20 | 0 |
| Expectations not met | 19 | 10 | 16 | 29 |
| Total | 100 | 100 | 100 | 100 |

between expectations and the three axial categories suggests that within the several career patterns, achievement levels, and value orientations there was sufficient latitude for most people to fulfill their expectations. Further analysis revealed that the individualistic type had a slight tendency to cite "conditions of work" as the aspect which fell short of their expectations. The leadership oriented appear more satisfied; a relatively high proportion stated that all their expectations had been exceeded. They mention particularly, as might be expected, income, status, and power. A relatively small proportion of the socially oriented group reported that their expectations had been exceeded; most of them stated that their expectations were met or that they were mixed. The elements of work which fell short of the expectations of this group were status and power.

What generalizations can be derived from the foregoing analysis of the role of expectations in the process of self-realization? The first and perhaps major finding is the high degree to which the expectations of the respondents with respect to their work had been fulfilled. About half could not think of any aspects of their work in which their expectations had not been met! It is unlikely that such a high proportion of the group would have had their expectations met if they had played a passive role in the process of their career determination and merely responded to external forces. A more probable explanation is that they played an active role in their career development and thus were actively involved in realizing the values and goals which they had set for themselves. We can say then that to a marked degree the respondents were successful in accomplishing their principal career objectives.

A substantial majority reported that their expectations had been met or exceeded in all or many regards. But if this finding is placed against the occupational status which they had been able to achieve we must conclude that many had had relatively modest expectations, particularly in view of their ability and training.

There are two possible explanations for this finding of modest expectations. First is that many had succeeded in moving outside the limited environment known by their parents, and this in itself was a difficult and challenging task. As young men, many had not known their own strengths and capacities and had no way of assessing what they would be able to accomplish after they left a familiar setting. The other explanation is that since they were intelligent and educated, they were able to assess realistically their ability as well as the world of reality and were less likely to have wild hopes than might less intelligent or less informed persons.

It may be that the report of the majority that their expectations had been fulfilled reflects in considerable measure this ability to face reality squarely and to incorporate the lessons of experience in evolving plans. They were able to modify their expectations as they realized that they could not be fulfilled. An indication of this is in the following account by a mathematician employed in industry who reported earnings of $25,000 annually. "My present job more than fulfills the intellectual and financial expectations I had when I got my Ph.D. It is short of expectations in the sense that I long for the extensive summer vacations of the academician. My work [also] falls short of some expectations I had as an undergraduate, in that my research has not entered the profounder branches of mathematics. By the time I got my Ph.D., however, I realized that the deepest aspects of mathematics would be beyond me, for I lacked the capacity for intense concentration over several years that their mastery would require. Once I recognized, or perhaps rationalized, this limitation, I formulated more modest goals, and it is these I am pleased to have exceeded considerably."

Further understanding of the process of self-realization can be acquired by considering the actions that individuals contemplate with respect to their work in the future. It can reasonably be assumed that those who have accomplished most of what they set out to do are much less likely to seek out or respond to alternatives than those who are dissatisfied with the way in which their careers have progressed.

In response to our query as to how long they expected to remain in their present job, two-thirds replied "permanently" or "indefinitely"; the remaining third indicated that they planned to leave at some time in the future. Answers to a further question, however, disclosed that only 12 percent of the entire group contemplated a radical shift to a new type of work. These two findings indicate that the majority have found the type of work that they prefer. At least they are reconciled to it. Many anticipate the possibility of shifting within their field in order to increase their income or otherwise to improve their situation. But even these individuals are not dissatisfied with their work situation—by and large their original, or revised, expectations have been met. The improvements that they contemplate are peripheral.

When we asked them to set down the changes they expected in the future with respect to their work (a somewhat less open-ended question), 72 percent replied that they expected to "continue in the same," 25 percent replied that they expected a "shift in emphasis," and only 3 percent expected a "substantial change." These answers reinforce the preceding findings. With minor exceptions, the members of the group do not contemplate any significant changes in their careers.

Among those who do expect some shift in emphasis in their work were the following: A priest who had been engaged in economic research reported, "I plan to move in the direction of more philosophical and less technical problems." A dean wrote, "I plan to return to full-time teaching." An operations research specialist in industry said that he expects to "get involved in research administration since there is generally somewhat more money given to a manager than to an individual contributor."

We asked the respondents to estimate the progress which they anticipate making over the next decade. Thirteen percent replied that they expected to have substantially the same duties and responsibilities. About half looked forward to increased responsibilities and rewards. The remainder, about a third of the total, looked forward to "substantially increased recognition and reward." A relatively higher proportion of those in the broad career pattern and in the lower achievement level look forward to marked improvement over the next decade. Each of these feels, but for different reasons, that his career is still open and that he has some way to go before he reaches his ceiling.

We also asked the respondents what kinds of changes in their work and careers might occur in the more distant future, that is, during the next ten to twenty years. Their replies indicated that they expected even fewer changes in the more distant future. Only about 1 in 6 looked forward to further advances in rank after the first decade, and an even smaller percentage, about 1 in 10, anticipated other changes, such as significant increases in responsibilities or rewards. We see then that those who expect changes to occur in their work situation assume that they will take place in the near future. Because such a high proportion of the group is in academic life, this estimate is a realistic one, since if they are to achieve the rank of full professor, they will probably be promoted within the next decade.

The following quotations help to explain why a considerable number do not expect to make much, if any, additional progress. A technical superintendent: "The next step would be plant manager . . . I have probably progressed at too slow a rate to attain this step." A distinguished sociologist: "I am now formally at the top rank; I have turned down administrative positions such as chairmanship and others. Therefore no financial advancement." Much the same reason was presented by a professor of geochemistry: "A full professor cannot be 'advanced.' He can change his position to an administrator, one with more pay, but this is not necessarily an advance professionally."

Most of those who are lower in the academic hierarchy

expected to be promoted either in the immediate future or within five years. A considerable number looked forward to moving to "a better community." A teacher who was also an author stated, "With each succeeding book published I expect to find myself more established as a writer." And a free-lance musician looked forward to more recognition as a result of "broadened opportunities as a solo artist and from appearing on TV." A social scientist in a nonprofit organization looked forward to having "more explicit policy responsibility within the next three years."

In their replies the respondents gave us a great deal of information about the way they had handled various career alternatives. This material provides additional understanding of the process of self-realization. In answer to the question of whether they had ever considered changing their line of work, one-third replied affirmatively. It is more striking that two-thirds never even considered the possibility of changing; this indicates their satisfaction with the way in which their careers were unfolding. Some indicated that they found the narrowness of their work somewhat burdensome, and others were dissatisfied by the slow rate of their progress, but the proportion who even thought about changing their line of work was relatively small.

Those who reported that they had considered changing their work but had not done so explained their reluctance largely in terms of their intrinsic interests. Occasionally they reported that external circumstances were unfavorable. In replying to the question of why he had not changed his field of work after having seriously considered doing so, a professor who turned down a lucrative offer in industry said, "The feeling that my field is biochemistry and I would be wasting my previous training and experience." Another who considered leaving academic life finally decided against

it because of his "conviction that teaching was a more rewarding and satisfying activity for me." Sometimes the
balance between present and future gains ruled against a
change as in the case of a man who refused a good position
for "fear of being stuck in a post with little appeal in itself
except as a possible stepping stone. Turned down offer."
Others balked at the conditions surrounding a possible new
job, such as the respondent who reported that he failed to
make a change because "it would have necessitated continuing to live in the New York metropolitan area." Another
said that the "money was not comparable."

Speculation about changing one's occupational choice or
career is quite different from actually responding to concrete attractive alternatives. About half of the respondents
indicated that they at one time or another had faced an
attractive career alternative. Only about one-third of this
group indicated however that they had *any* regrets about
not having pursued the alternative. Some realized that they
would probably be making more money had they shifted,
but they questioned whether on balance they would have
been in a better position.

An English professor who might have become a musician
reported, "Emotionally the narrowness of the usual musician's life repelled me; also I had no superabundant talents.
*No regrets.*" A research adviser to a foreign government
wrote, "I could have done more research with another
government department but I thought the group was biased.
*Regrets:* They turned out to be the best group." An industrial chemist who had once considered both law and medicine explained, "Lack of sufficient educational guidance and
pure chance. *Regrets:* Yes, chemistry is a frustrating and
unrewarding profession, socially and financially."

A curator of a library gave up teaching because of the

"seduction by a persuasive employer." He added that "I miss the students and the academic calendar." A newspaper copy editor considered a job in public relations but decided against it: "I don't like the work, believing that a great deal of it was false and harmful. *No regrets.*"

These examples indicate the wide range of opportunities that many in the group had at some point in their career, the reasons which led them to turn them down, and how they now feel about their earlier decision. As with all retrospective and prospective responses, they probably reveal more about the individual's present mood than about his past or future. But they do help to illuminate the process of self-realization in several important regards.

The first and perhaps most important point is that most of the group are pursuing the type of careers and work that they prefer. A minority feel that they have not yet reached the level of achievement and rewards which they consider commensurate with their ability, training, and age, but most of them expect to arrive there in the near future.

The second finding is that with the exception of a minority who are in the lower achievement levels, most respondents do not anticipate any significant changes in their future work or career. They expect their careers to remain not static, but stable. They have laid the foundations for a deepening or broadening in their work, and they expect to achieve this. They look forward to more responsibility and more status. But they are satisfied with respect to the basic nature of their work, and they do not see major changes ahead.

Many had opportunities to shift careers, but they let them go. In retrospect, some have regrets. But the regrets are mild. Some respondents indicate a desire for more adventure, excitement or recognition. These are able people, many of them very able. Some convey the impression that they are somewhat regretful that they will not be able to accomplish everything in the one career they have chosen.

The fourth finding relates to the importance of intrinsic determinants in the shaping of careers. The respondents were interested in such external considerations as income, but they placed a much higher priority on finding work in harmony with their interests, their desire for self-expression, and their need for freedom. These were the primary values and goals that they sought to realize. It was these internal constellations that gave direction to their efforts to shape a career, and for the most part they succeeded in meeting their personal needs and desires.

So far the process of self-realization has been analyzed solely from the vantage point of expectations and their fulfillment. Further understanding can be gained by recognizing explicitly that self-realization presupposes some anticipating concept of oneself in the future. Important in this connection is the fact that the *self* becomes the focal point. It is not "what the future will be like," but rather, "what *I* want to be like in the future, what *I* want to be doing, what kind of life *I* want to lead."

We must first attempt to understand the reasons back of the projection of a self-image into the future. It appears to be grounded in the individual's need for a reference point for assessing his needs and desires which cannot all be satisfied in the present. Since the nature of the developmental process itself dictates that the individual will have to live with the consequences of his actions, he must find some method of checking and controlling his wishes. If the individual is able to conceptualize what he wants to be in the future, he acquires a major organizing principle which can give direction and provide continuity to what would otherwise be random and unrelated actions. This organizing, directing, and controlling effort does not necessarily mean that his current impulses and needs are frustrated; only that the immediate gratification of some of them is postponed. The major challenge that individuals experience in the shaping of their careers is to handle their strong needs and desires in such a fashion that they do not disrupt their other important objectives and goals.

Our second effort must be to explore how the projection of self-image into the future occurs. Most people set objectives and goals that are related to what they have known during their formative years. They may want to rise a rung or two on the income or occupational ladder above that of their parents, but they seldom strive for much more. They may increase their expectations as they go along and as they find and test themselves. But adults, unlike children, do not usually hold on to fantasies. The grown individual is able to review and revise his image of himself as a result of what he learns about himself and about reality. It is not easy for the young person to have a clear perspective about his interests, capacities, and values. These become known to him only as he remains open and responds to the various influences that he encounters during the process of development. And this is the way he acquires knowledge of the opportunities that exist in his environment as well as the limitations and barriers which he must surmount. During this process he is subject to influences and pressures exerted on him by key persons in his environment, from his parents when he is young, and later from his teachers, his employers, and his connubial family.

Substantial differences are found in the extent to which individuals are able to project their self-image into the future, differences that appear to be tied to the depth of their commitments. But no matter how sharp or vague these projections are, they are generally open to adjustment and revision. An individual who starts with rather modest goals may find himself very successful and may revise his expectations upwards, sometimes radically. He may of course leave them intact. Another individual, who discerns a growing gap between his original goals and his ability to realize them, is likely to alter the projection of his self-image in order to avoid continuing disappointment.

Each person must develop a strategy which will enable him to tie the present to the future so that the decisions which he makes today will enable him to move toward realizing what he hopes to be tomorrow. This strategy, which is directed towards work and career, transcends these areas and encompasses the whole of a man's life plans. In turn the factors that shape the strategy also go beyond the specific elements involved in the development of a career. For the whole of a man's personality is involved here. His image of what he wants to be in the future will be affected by his self-confidence. His efforts to implement his strategy will be affected by his ability to take risks and his manner of responding to defeats. His capacity to postpone pleasure, his openness to new experiences and people, and his tolerance for ambiguity will all play a role both in what he ventures and in what he foregoes.

We have described self-realization as if it were a fully conscious process. Actually much of what transpires is not known to the individual either at the time it is happening or even in retrospect. Of course time is likely to unveil some elements which were originally shrouded because the individual was too involved to perceive connections or too inexperienced to be able to assess them correctly. In many instances a person learns most about the process of self-realization from the alternatives which he encounters. In responding to them he will perceive more clearly what he desires his future role to be as well as what he does not want to be or become. The choices that he is forced to consider play a crucial role in the process of self-realization. So do the key persons in his environment who can serve as models. They help to give concreteness to choices that might otherwise remain illusive.

# 10

# Life Styles

We have noted earlier that people must make crucial decisions with respect to their work and careers in their early and middle twenties, at a time when they confront other important challenges. During those years men may be called to serve in the Armed Forces, they consider marriage, they may already have a wife and children. Many young men face these new and demanding challenges at almost the same time that they must resolve whatever issues remain open with respect to their occupational decisions.

We have considered only one of these adult confrontations—military service. We must now consider the interplay between career development and the connubial family and between the time and effort directed to a career and that devoted to the other activities adults engage in—social, religious, political, recreational—for the way a man approaches the shaping of his career influences and in turn is influenced by these other important aspects of his life. Moreover, in contemporary society, most men eventually reach an age of optional or compulsory retirement. How they think about and how they eventually act in this matter of retirement provides yet another link between their work and life plans.

For many generations social scientists have studied men

at work but only occasionally have they broadened their approaches to take account of the aspirations and plans of workers after they stop working. Moreover, in their study of work, most social scientists seldom have a purview that includes the totality of an adult's life. While the job a man holds and the income he earns help shape the totality of his life, it is also true that in turn the type of life he seeks to lead will significantly determine how he works and how he uses his time off the job as well as his relationships to his family and the community.

This chapter will explore the relationships between the occupational development of the members of our group and three basic dimensions of their lives: their families, their activities off the job, and their retirement plans. In this way, we will open up, although we cannot exhaustively study, these important dimensions of career and life plans and their interaction.

The first assumption that we can formulate is that whether a man marries, when he marries, when he starts to have children, how many children he has, are all meaningfully related to the intensity of his career commitment and his occupational success. A wife and children are important new sources of gratification for a young man. But they are more than that. They make demands on him as a husband and father, demands which affect the use which he makes of his time, his energy, and the direction of his talents. What he does with his occupational capital can no longer be determined solely by his occupational objectives. He must also take into consideration his family responsibilities.

When a man has children, his occupational development may undergo basic transformation for children permit a man to extend his planning beyond the limits of his own life. They provide him with a second chance to realize his goals.

Many men, therefore, are willing to make radical alterations in their occupational plans when they have children. They see work as more than an opportunity for optimizing their own talents; they now seek also to take into consideration the educational and other developmental opportunities which they want to provide their offspring.

Nine out of 10 of our respondents were married and of this group 9 out of 10 were married before their thirty-third birthday. The surprising fact is that despite the interruption of their career by military service and the elongation of their studies, the age at which they married was only slightly higher than that of the average educated person.

A first indication of a possible relationship between marriage and career is provided by Table 30. We can see that those in the variant pattern are more likely to remain single or to marry later than those in the other patterns. At this point we cannot say whether those who are uncertain about what they want to be are unwilling to make an early marital decision; whether those who do marry early find it much more difficult to move away from the line of work in which they find themselves; or whether a man who marries early also knows early what he wants from work.

TABLE 30. *Age at first marriage and career pattern, in percent* (N = 333)

|  | Career Pattern | | |
| --- | --- | --- | --- |
| Age | straight | broad | variant |
| 18–23 | 26 | 26 | 11 |
| 24–29 | 53 | 47 | 50 |
| 30–35 | 7 | 14 | 23 |
| 36 or over | 4 | 4 | 2 |
| Never married | 10 | 9 | 14 |
| Total | 100 | 100 | 100 |

We may gain some clarification by considering the relationships between the age at marriage and achievement level. This is set out in Table 31.

TABLE 31. *Age at first marriage and achievement level, in percent* (N = 333)

| Age | Achievement Level | | |
| --- | --- | --- | --- |
| | *upper* | *intermediate* | *lower* |
| 18–23 | 32 | 23 | 15 |
| 24–29 | 49 | 48 | 55 |
| 30–35 | 7 | 14 | 13 |
| 36 or older | 6 | 3 | 4 |
| Never married | 6 | 12 | 13 |
| Total | 100 | 100 | 100 |

Here the relationship is easier to discern. Those in the top achievement level are more likely to marry very young. A much smaller proportion of those in the lower achievement level had married before their twenty-fourth birthday. It should also be noted that a relatively small proportion of the single group was in the top achievement level. It would appear that lack of responsibility for wife and children did not assure that a man would be successful in his career.

We might expect a close relationship between the value

TABLE 32. *Age at first marriage and value orientation, in percent* (N = 271)

| Age | Value Orientation | | | |
| --- | --- | --- | --- | --- |
| | *individualistic* | *leadership* | *social* | *ideological* |
| 18–23 | 26 | 25 | 16 | 21 |
| 24–29 | 49 | 51 | 61 | 43 |
| 30–35 | 8 | 10 | 14 | 14 |
| 36 or older | 5 | 2 | 4 | 15 |
| Never married | 12 | 12 | 5 | 7 |
| Total | 100 | 100 | 100 | 100 |

orientation of people toward their work and their age at marriage, but the data (Table 32) do not support this.

Considering the three major axes, we find one real surprise in the data. We might have postulated that those who married early would have been impeded in their careers by their additional responsibilities. But this was not so. The most successful tended to marry early, and those who had difficulty launching their careers, those in the variant pattern, tended to marry late. Single men, moreover, were not conspicuous among those in the top achievement level. Those who remained single did not make a differentially greater investment in their careers, were less talented, or may have had personality problems.

Since many men were aided financially in graduate school by wives who worked, it may be that it is the birth of the first child, rather than marriage, that has a significant influence on a man's career. For the birth of a child makes it impossible for most women to keep on working, and the support of the family falls to the man. Therefore let us see whether the age at which the members of the group had their first child played a part in their later occupational development.

As we might have expected, the data reveal that the age at which the respondents became fathers is in large measure a reflection of their age at marriage. Again the detailed data show that men in the variant pattern are the only group distinctive in this regard. They tend to have their children late. The relationships with achievement levels are much sharper. Those in the top achievement level have their first child early and those in the lower achievement level have their first child late or remain childless. Once again, the analysis in terms of the age of the respondents at birth of first child and their value orientations fail to reveal any significant relationships. The one tentative generalization emerging from this analysis is that the advent of the first child, even if the father is still quite young, does not appear to interfere with his career development.

A further analysis was undertaken to discover whether there is a significant relation between the number of children a respondent had and the three axial categories. With respect to career patterns, no significant relationship was found. In the case of achievement levels, those at the top were much more likely to have several children while those at the bottom tended to have no children or only one child. But the sharpest differentiation was found among the value types. The data are presented in Table 33.

TABLE 33. *Number of children and value orientation, in percent* (N = 249)

| Number of Children | Value Orientation | | | |
|---|---|---|---|---|
| | *individualistic* | *leadership* | *social* | *ideological* |
| 0 | 18 | 9 | 4 | 15 |
| 1 | 14 | 13 | 18 | 0 |
| 2 | 35 | 42 | 30 | 31 |
| 3 | 24 | 20 | 32 | 15 |
| 4 or more | 9 | 16 | 16 | 39 |
| Total | 100 | 100 | 100 | 100 |

A significant minority of the individualistic type had no children while a strikingly high proportion of the ideological type had four or more. It is interesting to note that there was a slow but consistent increase in the average number of children per family from one or two in the individualistic type to two or three in the ideological type.

We might have expected a relationship between value orientation toward work and size of family, but we would not have expected to find a relationship between age at marriage and achievement level, or between the age at which a man becomes a father and his success in his career. In our group, the more successful married earlier and started their families early. The cause of these relationships remains hidden. We shall, however, propose in the next chapter a few assumptions about what may lie behind these facts. Aside from these connections below the surface, there are of course relationships between work and family that enter into the conscious process of career decision-making.

The ways in which marriage can strengthen a man's motivation to succeed as well as increase his motivation to perform are suggested by the following excerpts. The dean of a graduate school said that marriage and a family "intensified my drive and ambition." The manager of public information for a large industrial concern said that marriage "aided [my career], gave more impetus to succeed and to provide an example for my children." A man who had floundered in the early part of his career reported, "My wife encouraged me to return to college teaching and generally assisted me in going back and finishing a Ph.D." A successful lawyer turned business executive wrote, "I believe my wife definitely contributed to my personality development by helping me overcome an innate shyness and bolstered my ego, thus giving me a great deal more self-confidence than I formerly had." A senior magazine editor said, "We have collaborated on juvenile books and my wife has often aided me directly in my work particularly during the years with the American Red Cross. She also worked during the months I free-lanced."

As we have noted, marriage often initially made it easier for a man to realize his career goals. A distinguished sociologist: "Marriage helped, since my wife worked and supported me for a time." An entomologist: "Because of our joint income I was able to remain in basic research and could afford to decline more lucrative jobs in industry." A TV executive: "My wife's work enabled me to take a chance on leaving academic life and trying to enter the radio-TV field. In other words, my wife supported me in this period."

On the other hand there were those whose wives and children interfered with their realizing their career objectives. An educational administrator wrote, "My wife was neglected as a child and has been very demanding on my time in ways that interfere with efficiency during work time. . . . Also I feel torn between family and work and unable to satisfy either. [This has] created extensive conflict situation."

Another kind of conflict was reported by a man who had had a good beginning teaching post at one of the nation's leading universities; he had left it to go to Israel "because my first wife insisted on the move. I was not Jewish and although I found Israel very interesting I found that it was really not the proper place for me. When I returned to the U.S.A. I had little money and had to take what I could get. I felt that a career in college teaching had been more or less forfeited."

Various types of restrictions follow upon marriage and children. A college dean: "It is possible that the responsibilities of marriage and parenthood immediately after the war may have slowed down my completing my Ph.D." A governmental official: "At present I have a big job offer from the U.N. but hesitate to bring the family to live in that bloody awful city. I live now in a spacious virtual paradise." A political science professor: "I once refused an attractive offer at a Midwestern university in part because of the age of my children." A professor of anthropology now teaching in the North: "I shifted employment from South to North in 1958 in *part* because I did not want my children to grow up in a world suffused with racial prejudice. But I intend to leave in *part* because a big city is no longer a place to raise a family." A successful Canadian lawyer outlined the reason for shifting away from politics: "The effect of a political career upon my wife and children, particularly the time I would necessarily be away from home, and the standard of living and security which I would not be able to provide, was a powerful factor in persuading me to give up this aspiration." The overriding importance of family and children was made most clear in the following comment of a professor of commerce at a college in one of the Southern states: "We would not locate anywhere that did not have first-rate medical and dental facilities. Also we want to be in or near good shopping. Also we need a top-rate community. Family considerations are basic to all other considerations."

Career goals were sometimes affected by the need for additional income to meet essential family needs. A professional man turned business executive wrote about his shift: "The financial responsibility for a wife and for children played a part in my decision to leave the law and go into business since one of the inducements was better present and future financial rewards in business." A research scientist explained his shift of jobs: "Increased income growth potential to finance education of children." A college administrator shifted from an institution which was having trouble raising money to one which was having pronounced success. He wrote, "I was also offered a pay increase of better than 20 percent, something that was very welcome in light of my big family."

Table 34 summarizes the replies from the respondents assessing the impact of their marriage on their career according to the first major axis—career patterns. Since 14 percent reported that marriage had had no effect, it is a tabulation of the replies of the 6 out of 7 in the married group who reported positive or negative effects.

TABLE 34. *Effects of marital status and career pattern, in percent of responses* (R = 314)

|  | Career Pattern | | |
|---|---|---|---|
|  | *straight* (R = 180) | *broad* (R = 87) | *variant* (R = 47) |
| Positive effects | | | |
| Motivation and moral support | 17 | 18 | 19 |
| Life more satisfying | 23 | 20 | 21 |
| Higher financial goals | 13 | 10 | 15 |
| Negative effects | | | |
| Marital problems | 6 | 3 | 13 |
| Restrictions | 32 | 38 | 15 |
| Increased financial need | 9 | 11 | 17 |
| Total | 100 | 100 | 100 |

The first finding that can be extracted is that in each of the three career patterns the positive and negative effects of marriage on careers were approximately equal. Many of the respondents singled out for particular emphasis the restraints on their careers that they felt as a result of marrying and having children. The only significant findings differentiating the three career patterns was the relatively smaller proportion of the variant pattern who complained about restrictions resulting from their marriage and the somewhat higher proportion who reported increased financial need and marital problems.

Table 35 pursues the analysis in terms of achievement levels. Once again few significant differences emerge. Those in the lowest level reported relatively fewer restrictions as a result of being head of a family. This may reflect, however, the earlier finding that they were more likely to remain childless or to have only one child.

TABLE 35. *Effects of marital status and achievement level, in percent of responses* (R = 314)

|  | *Achievement Level* | | |
| --- | --- | --- | --- |
|  | *upper* | *intermediate* | *lower* |
| Positive effects |  |  |  |
| Motivation and support | 16 | 18 | 20 |
| Life more satisfying | 26 | 21 | 19 |
| Higher financial goals | 9 | 13 | 15 |
| Negative effects |  |  |  |
| Marital problems | 2 | 6 | 9 |
| Restrictions | 33 | 36 | 24 |
| Increased financial need | 14 | 6 | 13 |
| Total | 100 | 100 | 100 |

Table 36 relates value orientations toward work and the effect of marital status.

Once again little of significance emerges, particularly since the number in the ideological type is too small to permit us to extract meaning from the data about this group. Those in the individualistic type selected significantly more of the positive effects of marriage on their career than did those in the leadership and social types.

TABLE 36. *Effects of marital status and value orientation, in percent of responses* (R = 314)

| | *Value Orientation* | | | |
| --- | --- | --- | --- | --- |
| | *individualistic* | *leadership* | *social* | *ideological* |
| Positive effects | | | | |
| Motivation and support | 16 | 18 | 20 | 25 |
| Life more satisfying | 26 | 16 | 13 | 38 |
| Increased financial need | 14 | 15 | 12 | 0 |
| Negative effects | | | | |
| Marital problems | 6 | 6 | 4 | 8 |
| Restrictions | 29 | 36 | 34 | 25 |
| Increased financial need | 9 | 9 | 17 | 4 |
| Total | 100 | 100 | 100 | 100 |

The only other point that emerges is the relatively heavy weight that the social type placed on the negative effects resulting from financial need.

While it was difficult to discern many significant relations between family and career from the foregoing tables, a few findings did emerge. More undoubtedly remain hidden. For instance, it would be necessary in a more elaborate investigation to distinguish the specific family circumstances, such as the problems presented by children, before assessing the respondents' replies concerning such matters as restrictions on their careers because of increased financial need.

Another way of studying career development is to relate what men do at work to their activities off the job. It was pointed out earlier that one of the important social transformations under way is the continuing decline in the number of hours that people are required to work at their jobs per day, per week, per year. During this century a large block of time has been recaptured by the individual to dispose of as he sees fit. Some stretch the length of their working day. But most people make other use of this "free" time.

They may use some of this free time in activities that are related to their jobs, such as the scientist at a university who does some corporate or governmental consulting, or the lawyer who is active in politics, which in turn provides him with additional legal work.

A second use of free time can be in connection with one or another type of community work, including religious, social, or political activities, in which the individual participates without seeking any specific occupational advantage. On occasion these turn out to be so demanding that they actually represent an obstacle to occupational success.

Free time can also be used in recreational pursuits and often this is a family affair. Many men spend their free hours on the golf links or the tennis courts, fishing, sailing, playing cards. A man may be a Sunday painter, play in a quartet, collect stamps, or engage in one of many other recreational activities.

The following analysis will assess the extent to which the use of free time is related to the career development of the members of our group. We will first consider activities related to work. Consulting for government, especially among a group of scientifically and professionally trained persons such as ours, is one way in which men make use of some of their free time. About one-third of our group engaged in governmental work other than regular employment, and many were involved in more than one governmental activity. About 3 out of every 4 consultants were paid for their services, although many of them also took on assignments for which they received no pay. Most of this work was for the federal government; a few respondents assisted state and local governments.

Many of the respondents, 3 out of every 4, engaged in some type of consulting or research work of a nongovernmental nature. Half of this group were active in more than one field. Most of them received money for this work although a significant minority did not. Consulting, writing, teaching, lecturing, and research—in that order—were the principal activities in which they engaged.

Also related to work were activities performed for professional societies. About 1 in 4 did not belong to such societies, and another quarter limited their activities to membership. But the other half were active as committee or panel members (25 percent), as officers (19 percent), or in educational work (6 percent).

The foregoing indicates that most of the group spent some of their free time, and many spent a considerable amount of their free time, in activities that were closely connected with their work.

The second area of activities in which our group engaged were community undertakings. Here the linkages to their work were less direct although sometimes they were there. Approximately 2 out of every 5 members of the group did not report any participation in community activities. Table 37 presents an overview of these activities.

The educational activities in which the group participated included acting as an elected or appointed official of the board of education and active membership in Parent-Teacher Associations. Activities on behalf of such bodies as the Civil Liberties Union, the NAACP, and other groups with a strong ideological commitment were included in

TABLE 37.  *Community activities, in percent of responses*
(R = 274)\*

| Type of Activity | | Percent |
|---|---|---|
| Religious | | 24 |
| Educational | | 22 |
| Local schools | 15 | |
| College alumni | 7 | |
| Civic and social | | 18 |
| Political | | 13 |
| Health and welfare | | 11 |
| Social service | | 10 |
| Cultural | | 2 |
| Total | | 100 |

\* 274 responses given by 167 respondents

what is subsumed under civic and social action. Those who were active in politics usually worked during election campaigns; a very few were committee members in a local political party. Health and welfare activities included raising funds for a hospital or leading a Boy Scout troop.

The use of leisure time is presented by type of activity in Table 38.

Only 1 in 6 did not list any leisure activity, but even this figure is probably too high. We can assume that even this 1 in 6 reads, goes to movies, or listens to music for pleasure. Of those who reported that they engaged in leisure activities, 95 percent listed more than one. Sports were the most popular; golf and swimming were reported most often, followed by tennis and fishing. Gardening and photography were among the favorite hobbies; woodworking, philately, and hi-fi were also frequently mentioned. Among the unusual activities engaged in were beekeeping, mead-making, and family genealogy. Participants in the

TABLE 38. *Leisure time activities, in percent of responses* (R = 456)*

| Type of Activity | | Percent |
|---|---|---|
| Sports | | 27 |
| Arts | | 21 |
|    Spectator and/or auditor | 11 | |
|    Active participation | 10 | |
| Hobbies and handicrafts | | 20 |
| Reading | | 10 |
| Home maintenance | | 5 |
| Cards and chess | | 4 |
| Travel | | 3 |
| Miscellaneous | | 10 |
| Total | | 100 |

\* 456 responses given by 234 respondents.

arts were, in order of frequency, musicians, painters, and actors.

A rough estimate was prepared of the amount of time our respondents devoted to the principal activities in which they engaged. This revealed that they were much more likely to make a major investment of time and energy in work-related or leisure activities than in community activities.

The participants were asked to assess whether their participation in any of these additional activities aided or hindered the development of their careers. Slightly more than one-third indicated that these activities had no particular effect. About the same proportion said that these activities had contributed to their career; only 5 percent indicated that they had hindered their progress, and an additional 12 percent reported mixed effects.

It was clear that our respondents considered these

activities a source of enrichment of their lives rather than a distraction with a deleterious effect upon their work. An inspection of our cross tabulation shows that most of those who considered these activities to be hindrances were in the variant pattern or were in the lower achievement level. Most of those in the top achievement level believe these activities have contributed to their careers.

The following quotations are a sample of the respondents' comments on their activities outside of work. A professor of Japanese: "Some of my free-lance activities have enhanced my reputation, and others have enabled me to meet various distinguished people. My acting experience contributed, I believe, to my success as a lecturer." A reporter: "Sports have given me a great self-confidence that has enabled me to roll with the punches. They have helped to raise my stature among news sources, fellow workers, and my chiefs." An academic: "Strangely, I have had more job offers in law teaching through people who had learned of me through musical activities than through my professional work."

A few reported adverse effects. A research chemist stated that his "divisional supervisor appears to feel that outside activities not directly connected with chemistry are bad." A general manager of an industrial company reported, "outside activities (largely 'do it yourself chores') may have influenced adversely development in direction of applied research and management rather than pure or basic research interests." A government research adviser who did not specify his activities but indicated that he engaged in them nightly (*sic*) said, "I have followed certain hobbies to the exclusion of work and job requirements which have suffered as a consequence."

Only 4 percent did not report participation in any type of work-related, community, or leisure activities. About two-fifths indicated that they participated in all three types of activities, and another third in at least work-related and leisure activities. Only 8 percent were active only in work-related and another 8 percent eschewed work-related activities completely.

The following picture emerges. Almost all of our group had sufficient time and energy to devote to activities that went beyond their job and work. However, much of their free time was spent on activities that were work-related. In general these contributed to the advancement of their careers, but occasionally they did not. They tended to spend less time in community and more in leisure activities. For most, these several activities in which they engaged had little or no direct effect on their careers. There were interactions between these activities and the respondent's career development, but it was rare that a man made such a poor distribution of his time and energy that he hobbled himself in his career. It was much more common for him to find some work-related activities that could help him in his career.

During this century men have not only recovered much time from their working day, week, and year, but they have also found themselves with years of leisure after retirement. While retirement was still a considerable way off for most of our group, we sought to explore their thinking about it since their responses would provide us with still another aspect of the style of life that they were shaping for themselves, not only now but for the future.

Somewhat over half (57 percent) expected to retire between 62 and 68 and another 13 percent after 68. Eight percent looked forward to retiring before they were 62 and the same percent said they expected never to retire. The remaining 14 percent did not reply to this question.

In response to a question as to what they planned to do after they retired, 2 out of 3 indicated that they would continue to engage in activities closely related to their work, such as the professor who said he planned to "continue writing after I stop teaching." Only 1 in 3 looked forward to leisure-type activities such as "traveling and enjoying grandchildren."

Those who planned to keep on working or to keep busy in work-related activities made comments such as the following. A professor of French: "Continue to write scholarly works—perhaps lecture at other universities." A government economist: "Research and writing, without teaching." A professor of architecture: "Continue study." A biochemist in a government laboratory said that he had "no plans. I hate inactivity and shall try to go on working in an emeritus capacity."

Others looked forward to a life of leisure. A professor of economics hoped to "travel and engage in civic activities." An industrial engineer wants to "travel, putter." A professor of English hopes to "lead the good life." A professor of chemistry envisions "research, learn radio operation, travel, maybe write, make a statue with polished oblong pieces of various woods, operate a way-out bookstore —no kidding."

Those who had experienced some difficulty with their careers, such as many in the variant pattern and in the lowest achievement level, were more inclined to expect to retire later or never, which suggests that they feel they need more time to achieve their goals. Those in the broad pattern who were still searching for a better work adjustment also looked forward to remaining at work for a long time. Consistent with what we have learned about the value types, those who were classified as individualistic were least inclined to expect to retire and those in the social type, who were more concerned with interpersonal relations than with their work per se, indicated that they would retire early.

Plans for retirement underscore once again the extent to which the majority of our group are work-oriented and find satisfactions from pursuing their careers along the lines they have set for themselves. Most of the group look forward to continuing to engage in activities closely related to their work even after they retire.

The preceding data have been able only to open up a consideration of the relations between work and life styles. We have considered three relationships: that of career development with marriage and family, with activities outside of work, and with the ideas that people have about retirement. In this section we will call attention to certain balancing mechanisms which may help to explain the manner in which people confront and resolve these relationships which are built into the lives of every adult.

From the vantage point of a man's work and career, outside activities can be used in one of three ways: as an extension and enlargement of the work activities from which he derives satisfaction and meaning, as a complementary area from which he can gain important satisfactions not directly derivable from his work, or as a compensatory area. To illustrate: the professor who spends most of his free time as a consultant to the federal government is engaged in *extension;* the successful physician who seeks a second creative outlet in painting is following a *comple-*

*mentary* approach; the unsuccessful businessman who devotes all of his free time to becoming an expert card player evidences a *compensatory* approach.

A man who is frustrated in his work may seek an outlet far afield, in religion or social activities or through the pursuit of a hobby from which he hopes to derive important satisfactions that he cannot find on his job. Were it not for this mechanism, there would be many more disgruntled people.

These several mechanisms which apply to outside activities also have relevance to marriage and the family. Many a husband and father who cannot exercise leadership on the job is able to act truly as the head of the household and thereby derives complementary gratifications. Others who realize that they are unlikely to be very successful in their work seek to compensate for these unfulfilled expectations by investing more of their energies in the training and development of their children. Many professional people achieve satisfaction through the process of extension: they provide guidance and counseling in the areas of their specialization not only to their immediate family but to many relatives and friends.

We see then that certain parallels can be found in the operation of these two mechanisms—in the use of free time and marriage and family relationships—but one important difference must be noted. Young people always have to make decisions about their free time in relation to their studies. But marriage is a new experience. Many men encounter difficulty in their marriage because they are no longer able to use their free time as in the past.

One of the less desirable aspects of the current scene is the extent to which work-time and free-time are merged, especially for many in corporate life. In order to move up the occupational ladder many men feel obliged to spend much of their free time with their peers and superiors, whether they want to or not. And many resent this, for it robs them of the freedom to work out their own ways of extending, complementing, or compensating for what occurs in the realm of work. It can be assumed that the value orientation of an individual will determine the nature of his response to this situation. One who belongs to the individualistic type may consider it a gross imposition; the social type may welcome it.

The ideas that people hold about retirement can also be considered from the point of view of balancing mechanisms. The contemplation of retirement is of course different from the contemplation of adulthood, for while adulthood represents a widening and deepening of opportunities for the young, retirement is linked to old age and ultimately death. For many people, although less for the members of our group, as we have seen, retirement also represents a sharp discontinuity with their earlier pattern. And most people fear discontinuity.

Most of our group did not hesitate to project themselves into the future to the time when they would no longer be regularly employed. A considerable number looked forward to carrying on, with some modifications, the same activities after retirement as they had before. They viewed retirement largely as an extension of their work lives. Others looked forward to engaging in pleasurable activities that they had long postponed. To them retirement would be a complement or a compensation for the restrictions and constraints of their years of active work.

The members of our group were able to incorporate

retirement into their projection of themselves into the future. They had sufficient intelligence, realism, and a sense of proportion for this forward look. Moreover, they were able to see retirement in positive terms. Many could expect, if they wanted to, to continue in the same line of work. Some had intellectual and psychological resources which would enable them to shift their activities. Others looked forward to having sufficient savings or income to be able to realize quite elaborate plans, including considerable travel.

We knew from the beginning of our investigation that career development could not be studied completely independently of other aspects of adult existence, but it was only in the course of our study of our data that we became more fully aware of the need to develop a framework that would include the whole of a man's life. The need for such a broadened framework is underscored by recent major changes in the social environment, such as higher per capita income, a longer and healthier life span, and fewer prescribed hours of work. The current situation is vastly different from what prevailed as recently as the beginning of this century when many worked from sun-up to sundown. In the world of tomorrow the relationships between the work and nonwork areas of life will be even more important for determining not only the life of the individual but also the quality of the society.

# Performance Potential

The point of departure of our study of the career development of a group of intellectually able young men was the search for factors that might help to explain their level of performance in the world of work. They had all demonstrated superior capabilities in graduate school. We wanted to uncover the reasons that led some to be much more successful in their careers than others. This chapter will synthesize what we have learned.

In addition, it will pursue another track. We knew that our group had unique characteristics which were reflected both in their advanced level of education and their occupational concentration in professional, technical, and managerial positions, but we expected that much of what we would be able to delineate about the shaping of their careers would have had relevance and pertinence for an understanding of the career development of other groups in the population. The weights of the individual factors might be different for different groups, but the underlying processes of career decision-making are probably largely the same. Therefore, we will attempt to describe the general processes involved in career development and suggest how the most important of them act and interact. In this we hope to make a contribution toward the formulation of a more general theory of career development. We cannot take more than a step in that direction but even a first step may prove helpful to those who follow.

Some studies of career development emphasize "luck," while others believe "emotional stability" is the determining factor. A word about each of these widely held opinions.

While luck, which is one way of describing the circumstances which lead one to be in a certain place at a certain time, may go far to explain the success of a particular individual, it is scarcely an adequate basis for a more general explanation of performance. Even when men are lucky, some pass up unique opportunities while others grab them. We know that many of those lucky enough to be born into families able to provide them with a wide range of opportunities are not particularly successful, while many others who grow up under disadvantageous circumstances are able to make an outstanding success of their careers. Luck explains either too much or too little to be a useful theory.

Much the same can be said about emotional stability. Emotional disturbance in an individual need not necessarily be associated with poor performance; it may be and often is connected with superior performance. Moreover, there is no clear-cut evidence that those at the top are more "normal" than those whose performance has been less distinguished. But most important is the fact that emotional factors represent but one facet of the total personality; there are many others such as capacity, interests, and values, which are clearly related to performance.

At a minimum, an adequate framework for the study of performance must be broad enough to encompass both the individual's characteristics, the reality situation in which he finds himself and, as we will see, the reactions between the two. While we can discount luck we cannot ignore such pervasive reality factors as the family into which one is born, the developmental opportunities available, the extraordinary demands that the society may make such as during war, the state of the job market when one enters it, and still other social determinants.

If then we tentatively consider as inadequate any monistic theory of career development it may be helpful to delineate the principal factors that do appear to have played a significant role in the early working lives of our respondents and summarize the part that each appeared to play in determining the level of performance.

To begin with, original endowment is of course crucial for the level of accomplishment that an individual eventually reaches. Other factors, circumstances, and conditions may play a major role in determining whether the individual makes optimum use of his endowments, and will unquestionably determine the direction he follows, but mental prowess counts; and to judge from our data it counts a great deal.

Second, the quantity and quality of the education and other preparation that an individual undertakes before he starts to work are also clearly important in determining differential performance. On a canvas large enough to encompass the entire labor force it can quickly be seen that without certain general and specialized types of educational preparation, individuals will be excluded from many preferred lines of work regardless of their basic endowment. While an occasional individual may overcome the handicap of limited schooling, the probability is that this will not happen. If handicapped by inadequate education, some will never be able to enter the race, and the question of their competitive performance will never be raised. But for those who prepare and train for professional or technical work, the opportunities and limitations that they encounter along their educational route will probably have an important influence.

Third is the ease or difficulty experienced in crystallizing occupational choice. If young people are unable to resolve this decision while in college, or if they experience difficulties in resolving it adequately, they will be without a rudder in steering their way through the complex and variegated educational opportunities which they encounter. They may flounder and consequently be retarded in getting launched on their careers. Some of those who flounder may later make up the lost time. Some who resolve their occupational choice early come to find after a few years at work that their solution was not the right one, and they are then back where they started. They must choose anew and prepare for a different career. This too sets them back, some permanently.

What people achieve in their work and career depends, fourth, in substantial measure on their motivation, attitudes, and values. Other things being equal, those who seek to achieve the most will in fact achieve more than those who are less inclined to invest as much in their work and in the pursuit of their careers.

Fifth, we have seen that the shaping of a career involves the individual in building bridges between the present and the future. He does this in part by constructing a system of expectations and by projecting himself into the future. This helps to direct and guide him as he moves from the present into the future. But men live not only with their ideas and ideals; they also must cope with the world of reality, which on occasion can prove that their expectations were either too high or too modest. Whenever a man's expectations are not fulfilled by reality, he must reassess them in order to bring them more in line with what he has come to learn about himself and the world in which he lives and works. Some men are more adept than others in profiting from their experiences and in adjusting their expectations when necessary. These men are more likely to be successful. Others may waste much of their substance running after illusions; still others may settle for too little.

Sixth, a man's wife and family can be a major source of support to him in his work or on the other hand can be the focal center for difficulties and disturbances that drain him of much of his enthusiasm, his energy, and his capacity. Many men are forced to invest so much of themselves in keeping conditions at home in tolerable balance that they have little left over for their work. Others of course can accomplish more at work because of the satisfactions and support that they realize at home. It can make a very great difference in a man's life for instance, whether his wife has a modest income of her own and is willing to use it to further his career, or whether she refuses to move to another city where her husband can get an excellent job.

Finally, men live in a world that transcends the limits of their job. They encounter many opportunities to gain satisfactions from activities that lie outside the area of their work. How they respond to these opportunities, whether they seek major gratifications from activities and relationships in the nonwork area, will have much to do with what they are able to accomplish in the world of work. While some reasonable investment of time and energy in nonwork activities can prove constructive in relation to work, preoccupation with this sector of life can easily lead to lessened accomplishment or even an unsuccessful career.

These then are the principal factors that were significantly related to differential performance as evidenced by the preceding analysis. With these as background, we sought to construct profiles of respondents in the different achievement levels. Those in the higher achievement levels had the following characteristics:

1. Outstanding grades in graduate school.
2. Resolution of occupational choice by junior year in college.
3. Early completion of education, including early doctorate.
4. Quick start and progression in careers.
5. Successful assumption of adult responsibilities, including military service, marriage, and family formation.

Following is the profile of those who were least successful in their careers.

1. Good but not outstanding marks in graduate school.
2. Uncertainty and delay in formulating occupational choice.
3. Delay in the completion of formal education, including a delayed doctorate or no doctorate.
4. Considerable floundering in early career.
5. Difficulties in responding to the demands and opportunities of adulthood including military service, marriage, and children.

While each of the foregoing differentiations appears to be independent of the others there may be a hidden underlying factor that gives shape and direction to the

careers and lives of these generally successful persons. It
may be useful to think of the factor as something akin to
Spearman's G-factor (G standing for general) in his theory
of intelligence. This factor or constellation is difficult to
describe or even outline, but it manifests itself in the individual's dealing successfully with all of the factors enumer-
ated as determinants of occupational success. Hence, we
propose to refer to it by the somewhat broad expression,
*performance potential*. This concept has in fact worked its
way into conventional language and thought; for example,
when we say, "he will go far," "he is slated for the top,"
or "he is presidential timber," we refer to certain qualities
which are not readily definable or specifiable, but which
are not simply equatable with endowment and which seem
to appear in retrospect. Sometimes observers are surprised
about an individual's actual performance because they had
not recognized his performance potential in advance.

Superior performance potential favors, but does not insure, a high level of performance. Conversely a low performance potential does not preclude eventual high level
achievement. The reasons for these caveats were suggested
earlier. Personality characteristics, among them the performance potential, represent only one set of determinants. A
second set are embedded in the social reality that the individual encounters during the course of his adult work and
life and against which his personality determinants are
played out. And the ways in which they are played out
constitute the third set of determinants.

Here are some of the major findings about the ways in
which social reality influenced the level of achievement of
the members of our group. We will summarize the findings
by setting out the circumstances that had a negative influence on career achievement.

Men whose fathers were in the lower occupational levels were more likely to be in the lower achievement levels; this probably reflects their reduced opportunities to acquire a superior education.

Those who secured their doctorates relatively late were likewise overrepresented among the lower achievers; sometimes this indicated a career deflection as they were forced to take jobs to earn money to complete their studies.

Those who served in the military services and never rose above enlisted rank were likely to be in the lower achievement level. Apparently failure to demonstrate leadership capacity in the military was indicative of some lack of initiative or force that also handicaps a man in civilian life.

Those who reported serious marital troubles were also more likely to be on the lower achievement level. Disturbances within the home apparently did not end there, but carried over into the work arena.

Numerous job shifts were also a negative indicator. Men who changed employers frequently were more likely to end up on the lower achievement level. Most men will not willingly leave jobs where they are relatively well paid and where the other conditions that they seek in work are satisfactory. Therefore those with multiple job changes probably had more than the average difficulty in the labor market. But irrespective of the reasons for frequent job changes, when a man looks for a new job his prospective employer will usually study his work record. A record of frequent changes is often a deterrent to securing a good job.

One other situation deterrent to high level achievement can be extracted from our earlier analysis. While our group contained a relatively small number of persons in the general category of creative artists—musicians, painters, authors—even this small number alerted us to the extent to which a poorly structured market for the services of these people exercises a negative influence on their career development. There are outstanding rewards for the exceptional, but only modest rewards for the merely talented. Facing an unresponsive market, it is not surprising that most of this group found themselves on the lowest achievement level.

The determinants anchored in reality cannot always be classified as clearly favoring or interfering with the development of a man's career. A generally negative constellation such as identified above may on occasion precipitate behavior that results eventually in the individual's performing at a high level. We encountered in our study many examples of men whose long period of military service afforded them an opportunity to reconsider their career, their values, and their goals. As a result of this opportunity for reconsideration, they sharpened their perspective and moved more purposefully to accomplish their new objectives. Serious illness forced one of our respondents to change his occupational choice. Required to remain sedentary, he developed a high specialized skill that he could fully exploit.

In summarizing this second set of determinants, we must point out their essential duality: the situations that people encounter during the course of their career development may provide them with opportunities or may place limitations and hurdles in their path. The strong demand for physicists that developed in the 1950s was a special opportunity; the lack of interest of the American public in the work of poets is a deterrent to the development of young creative writers.

Reality situations can also operate to make demands on individuals to which they can respond positively or negatively. The requirement that young men serve in the Armed Forces is a demand, but to some it can prove to be a constructive experience. On the other hand, if a young man is forced to remain on active duty for a very long time, he may feel pressure to shift his career goals because of the many years during which his plans are in suspension.

Some situations can result in stimulation; others have more of the quality of a temptation. When a lawyer, acting as house counsel, learns about the inside of a business, he may contemplate broadening his horizon and eventually shifting into work which will be both more demanding and more rewarding. But other situations which hold forth large immediate returns may present a temptation which the individual cannot withstand. Many a promising scientist was lured away from the research laboratory into lucrative administrative positions.

Finally, some situations provide support and encouragement to the individual in the pursuit of his career goals; others are fraught with danger and discouragement. There is the old adage that nothing succeeds like success. Some individuals find themselves in situations where they have an opportunity to use their ability fully, others in situations that lead to set-backs and failures. Several respondents indicated that they had at one time worked under supervisors who were incompetent or jealous and who had impeded their progress.

For analytical purposes situational factors in career development can be organized in terms of the following four dualities: opportunities and limitations, demands and pressures, stimulation and temptation, encouragement and discouragement. The significance of any particular situation will often depend less on its objective aspects than on the manner in which the individual perceives and responds to it.

We have seen that people differ as to their performance potential, but these differences alone do not suffice to explain differences in career development. People also confront a different social reality, but again these differences do not alone explain the differences in performance. How the reality is interpreted by the individual and how he responds to it is a portion of his total personality. We can single out certain tendencies in our group which we call response mechanisms and which are considered as a third set of determinants.

Just as objective situations assume highly subjective importance for different individuals, so the responses that people make to these situations can vary widely. In our approach to this third set of determinants—the responses that people make to the situations which they encounter—we face many of the same methodological difficulties that we confronted in trying to establish some order among the other sets of determinants of performance. Once again we will have to be satisfied with a partial rather than comprehensive analysis. Our effort will be devoted to delineating a limited number of response mechanisms that can be used to describe the process of interaction in a more systematic manner.

We were able to discern in our group three response mechanisms and to them we applied the following descriptive terms: investment, time perspective, and what we call the stance, whether it is active or passive. A word about each. Investment refers to the time and effort people are willing to put into their work. Time perspective is the short-range or long-range point of view that an individual takes toward his career. The third mechanism refers to the phenomenon that people can approach their careers by adopting and following either an active or passive stance.

While our materials enabled us to delineate these three mechanisms, the fact that we were unaware of their existence before we began our study limited the data at our disposal. However, we were able to make certain tentative conclusions.

The following findings bear on the investment mechanism. Men in the top achievement level gave clear evidence that they were heavily committed to the pursuit of their work and career goals. They were deeply involved in their work and made substantial investments of time and energy. They tended to start very early to devote themselves to their studies, and then to perform well in the work arena. One caveat is that a high degree of investment need not necessarily manifest itself in superior achievement.

Almost all of those who were classified as ideological types, irrespective of their achievement levels, gave unmistakable evidence of being deeply involved and exerting special efforts in the pursuit of their major goals. Since money and status were relatively low in their value scales, they were less likely to be found in the top achievement level, but their involvement and investment differed little from that of those who were assessed as the most successful.

There were also some relationships that can be suggested, if not demonstrated, between the time perspective and the differential performance of the members of the group. Those who had been able to determine their occupational choice early were more likely to be found in the top achieve-

ment level. This was also true of those who had been able
to finish their educational preparation early and particularly
those who earned their doctorate as expeditiously as possible. Those who fulfilled their military service requirement early were also in a stronger position to pursue their
career goals.

The relatively low achievement level of those in the
variant pattern reflected in some measure the costs of an
inadequate time perspective. Men who had difficulty in
getting started or who got started in the wrong direction
had to pay a big price because of the delay occasioned by
changed goals or changed jobs.

Subsumed under the concept of time perspective are
such considerations as the desirability of developing a proper
sequencing of one's career decisions, the recurrent need to
balance immediate against more distant satisfactions and
goals, the testing of reality, and the capacity to project oneself into the future and to know what one wants to be,
where one hopes to be, and when.

Successful career development also demands that one be
able to develop realistic expectations and then to revise
them upward or downward as reality requires. In our group
difficulties in effectively linking the present to the future
were likely to be reflected in a lower level of achievement.

A few relationships can also be suggested between our
earlier findings and the active-passive stance that people
adopt in relation to work and careers. Among those in the
broad pattern who were also in the top achievement level
were many who gave clear evidence of following an active
stance toward all matters affecting their work and career.
They not only responded to pressures from the outside but
also moved energetically to find and take advantage of op-

portunities that would enable them to further their career goals.

In contrast, included among those in the straight pattern on the lower achievement level were many who were passive with respect to their career development. They conveyed the impression of being in a particular groove and then being unable or unwilling to do anything other than continue in it, even though they might have improved their situation if they made some effort.

The most striking example of an active stance was found among those in the variant pattern who had reached the top achievement level. These were men who had made a wrong start, but as soon as they recognized their error they set about quickly to remedy it and succeeded in doing so.

Those who had served as officers in the Armed Forces were more likely to be in the top achievement level. A reasonable assumption is that the same active stance that helped these men advance in the military service also played a part in their success in civilian careers.

There is a strong suggestion in the materials that many who were classified as social types had a passive stance toward work. They were somewhat less successful in terms of our criteria, and they looked forward to retiring as early as possible.

The behavior of men with respect to their activities off the job also appears to be related to this active-passive stance. Those who were more likely to seek out and find work-related activities in their free time were more likely to be among those in the top achievement level.

Care must be taken not to confuse mere activity with an active stance; those who took an active stance were not necessarily those who engaged in the greatest amount of activity. Our data revealed that those in the top achievement level were much more likely to have had only one or two employers. Apparently those with a truly active stance toward work and career were able to appreciate that frequent changes in jobs might hinder rather than advance career prospects. Even a move to a job paying a higher salary or a shift into a position offering more prestige could prove in the long run to have a negative effect on one's career. Careful deliberation about whether to accept what appears to be a better job and a decision not to do so may be an indication of an active stance.

There are some additional conclusions of a more general nature suggested by the foregoing discussion of response mechanisms in career development. Closely associated with heavy investment appears to be a deepseated interest in a particular field or function. This interest contributes to the establishment of a need which can be fulfilled through certain types of work. Generally this need is likely to be satisfied through intrinsic aspects of work. Often however, a high order of investment is made because the individual's goals are concerned with such externals as the making of money or the achievement of higher status. The intensity of the need is what counts. Unless the individual has such a need, he is likely to seek more immediate satisfactions more readily available outside the area of his work.

The time-perspective mechanism helps the individual to structure and order the choices he must take. It helps him to relate what has gone before with the alternatives that he confronts and the goals that he hopes to achieve in the future. Without these linkages his actions would be without aim or purpose.

A related but distinct aspect of time perspective is the

way it operates to give the individual an opportunity to test
out, not once but repeatedly, his ability to realize the intermediate and long-range goals he has set for himself. Successful career planning requires that the individual obtain
confirmation from the environment in which he works that
he is on the right track, right at least to the extent that he
can overcome the obstacles in his path.

But time perspective is not merely an ordering mechanism.
It also contains the element of imagination, a key quality in
the shaping of a career. Imagination makes it possible for
the individual to see in dim outline what he might become
or accomplish in the future. And the pull of these future
goals can help him organize and mobilize himself more
effectively.

Time perspective also facilitates the individual's exercising
control over the demands for short-run gratifications. These
are always present and frequently very powerful. The individual needs support to be able to postpone or forego the
gratification of current needs and desires. Time perspective
also makes it possible for the individual to make sacrifices
in favor of a distant goal. Unless the distant goal can assume
a present value, the individual will not make sacrifices on its
behalf; time perspective helps the individual to raise his
tolerances to current frustrations.

The time-perspective mechanism encourages action, including the assumption of risks, directed toward achieving
distant goals. To assume considerable risk today is reasonable and possible only if one can count on substantial
rewards tomorrow.

The last mechanism, the active stance, implies that the
individual realizes that through his actions he can materially
affect the shape of his career and his level of achievement.

It is the antithesis of the position that what happens to one is solely a matter of luck. While no sensible person can ignore the fact that he must find the solution to his career problems in a real world—and that a real world establishes boundaries in the form of both opportunities and limitations—the key characteristic of the active stance is that the individual sees himself as capable of working on the situations he confronts and altering them at least in part in his favor.

In contrast, those who have a passive stance are much more likely to respond to external influences whether they are events or people, and to act only in response to a strong external influence. They do not attempt to create situations that they can manipulate to accomplish more readily their objectives.

Now two simplifying generalizations can be ventured. The first calls attention to the role of continuity in career plans and achievement. What happened in the past always exercises a strong and frequently a compelling influence on the present and the future. This helps to explain why careers often appear to be characterized by either a benign or a vicious cycle. We talk of lucky and unlucky people. Those who get off to a good start are likely to keep on in the same direction. For those who falter along the way, the outlook may not be favorable. The explanation of this tendency toward cumulation lies in the mutual reinforcement of the objective and the subjective. A favorable objective situation makes it easier for an individual to realize his more ambitious goals and as he begins to realize them, he finds himself in a better objective position to continue to do so. The success he has experienced adds to his confidence and conviction that he is heading in the right direction. The world has helped him confirm his concept of the self he has projected into the future, and this in turn makes it easier for him to realize it. The continuity-cumulation tendency gives new meaning to the adage—nothing succeeds like success.

The same cumulative sequencing can occur when short-comings and failures begin to follow one after the other. If the individual fails and fails again, he will soon lose his nerve, and this in turn makes it more difficult if not impossible for him to pursue his career goals.

The second generalization refers to the way motivation (or the subjective factors generally) and environment can be considered functional equivalents in the structuring of a person's behavior with respect to his career. We all know of the exceptional person who, when confronted by what appear to be unsurmountable obstacles, can overcome them by an act of will—by determination, drive, and work. But we also know that a high proportion of the people who reach the top come from backgrounds which were relatively supporting and encouraging. These two conventional pieces of wisdom can be more readily understood within the context of the generalization which sees motivation and environment as functional equivalents. The individual with substantial drive can overcome a greater number and more severe environmental hardships. The person with less drive may reach the top if he receives strong support. Motivation and environment, while discrete phenomena, can act at times as rough equivalents in the realization of long-range career goals.

The sketch of a comprehensive framework for the study of career development just outlined provides the basis for developing answers to three crucial issues in the field of career development: why individuals with equally good endowment frequently perform at quite different levels; why talented persons facing the same objective situations respond differently with consequent different impact on their later careers; and why men with quite different personality characteristics are able to perform at the same high levels.

To find adequate answers to these and other important career questions requires an elaboration of the foregoing matrix. There is need for further research along several axes. The first involves a deepening of the approaches for delineating and evaluating personality elements. New methods are required to probe reality situations, particularly the way in which they operate to open opportunities or set limitations. There is also a need for the systematic study of response mechanisms through which people establish the sequences and continuities—and sometimes the shifts—out of which their careers are shaped and their level of performance achieved. The final challenge is to explore more thoroughly the concept of the performance potential. More systematic analysis could lead to concretizing this elusive but suggestive concept which appears to provide one important key to the understanding of personality factors in performance.

# The Conservation of Talent

Our primary goals in this research undertaking were to discover new knowledge about the career development of a group of talented persons and to elaborate a systematic framework for the study of the career itself. Our point of departure was the talented individual and his search for a place in the world of work. Although our primary focus was on how the individual seeks to shape his career, we knew that this process plays itself out in the external world which provides both opportunities and barriers.

In this concluding chapter we will consider the impact of three dimensions of this external world on career development. The first is the current educational and guidance structure as it facilitates or retards the optimal development of talent. Second, we will review the manner in which specific work environments in corporate enterprise, academic institutions, and government influence the utilization of talent. Finally, we will review certain broad social policies such as compulsory military service, the maintenance of high level employment, and the pattern of social expectations as they affect the conservation of talent.

Our society has become increasingly dependent on people whose talents, skills, and competences have been developed to a high order. And our society has become so structured as to enable people with talent to make effective use of their specialized abilities. Many changes have been made in the society that the Founding Fathers envisioned and planned for, which was primarily composed of independent yeomen, small numbers of craftsmen, and still smaller numbers of merchants and professional people.

Today there are more men and women employed in professional, technical, and managerial positions than there are farm workers and craftsmen. And this group is growing more rapidly than any other sector.

Although earlier societies did recognize the importance of talent, only a very few individuals actually reached high orders of excellence in religion, statecraft, military affairs, humanities, or the arts. These earlier societies reached their highest levels of accomplishment through the contributions of the talented few, but the work of the philosophers, writers, and artists was only peripherally related to the mundane tasks performed in everyday life by the majority of the population. The essential difference between these earlier societies and our own is that they were sensitive and responsive to the one man in a million, while we must be concerned with the education and training of multiple millions of professional and technical persons. Other societies have been responsive to genius, but since genius is unique, it can be recognized and honored but cannot be produced. Talent, however, is much more widely distributed among the population, and the conditions that govern its development and utilization can have a much more direct and specific effect on the progress and welfare of these societies.

A society that recognizes its dependence on the many who are talented and trained rather than the very few whose genius develops idiosyncratically must pay particular attention to the process which determines the way people acquire competence and skills. For a professional or technical training takes twenty or more years and increasingly requires continuing efforts to maintain competence throughout the whole of a man's career. The educational process, then, stands in a crucial relationship to an advanced industrialized society. The quality and number of persons who acquire competence depends on how effectively the schools perform their mission. It is therefore appropriate to begin a discussion of a policy for the conservation of talent by considering our findings that bear specifically on education and guidance.

Let us look at the financial outlay involved in this education for the professions, for academic work, and for the higher positions in business, government, and nonprofit organizations. For many years local and state governments have assumed the burden of financing elementary and secondary schooling; they have also underwritten, but much more selectively, the costs of college and graduate instruction. Since the end of World War II, the federal government has developed a multiplicity of programs aimed at covering the direct costs incurred by many who pursue advanced studies. In addition, colleges and universities have broadened the amount of scholarship and fellowship aid—and loans—that they have been able to extend.

But certain untoward developments must be set against these favorable trends in financing education. In many urban communities the elementary and secondary school systems are so mediocre that a small but increasing proportion of parents feel obliged to enroll their children in private schools. This means that the financial burden of education is very substantial even before a young person enters college.

Moreover, the rise in tuition and in the costs of room and board has been very rapid during the postwar years. The elongation of the educational process has added to the costs. Two or three years in military service further delays the completion of a young man's developmental cycle and postpones the day when he can become fully self-supporting.

There is no need to elaborate the foregoing. While those who successfully complete advanced education and training are eventually in a better position to earn higher incomes, the hard truth remains that many are unable to finance such a long and costly preparation or can do so only by deflecting valuable time and energy away from their studies to earn money to help defray their expenses.

We were impressed, time and again, by the number of our respondents who had to devote much time to odd jobs while in college or graduate school to pay for their education. And we were equally impressed by the number who were able to continue their education only through the aid extended by the GI Bill.

From the point of view of policy there still are a large number of financial barriers to the fuller development of the nation's talent. Many able young people, especially from homes where college has been beyond the family purview, early make decisions about their educational and occupational future that preclude college. Some make this decision on the basis of incorrect information; they could, in fact, secure the necessary financing. Others are probably correct in estimating that the financial burden, even if they could have it underwritten, would be more than they are willing to shoulder. While financial barriers interfere less with the continuity of education of able people at the higher ranges of the educational hierarchy, losses are substantial, especially among the large numbers who have interests in the arts, humanities, medicine, and many of the social sciences where governmental and other fellowship funds for advanced study remain relatively small.

There is much to be said in favor of the argument that tax dollars should be used to make educational opportunities available for each individual to develop his competences to the optimum. But important as education is, there are other basic individual and social needs, including health, defense, social welfare, and research, which require government funds. Available government funds have not been adequate to cover these priorities. While, as we have seen, government has historically met a substantial part of the direct costs of elementary and secondary education in the United States, students and their families and philanthropy have covered much of the costs of higher education. Since those who acquire a higher education are likely to have substantially higher earnings, the pressure on them to cover part if not all of the direct costs of their education is not contra public policy.

The crucial point here is that no individual who has the capacity and desire to proceed with his education should be blocked by lack of funds. Those without financial resources should have access to educational opportunities through free tuition, scholarship aid, or loan funds. Even then these students would have financial problems. Tuition is but one part of the cost of education. Living expenses are a second major component. Earnings foregone are a third. We saw that many in our group were handicapped in the pursuit of their doctorate because they had to support themselves and their families. With the constant elongation of education and with compulsory military service, many able young people must delay marriage and particularly having children until they are in their thirties—or find other means of support. A realistic policy must bring these additional dimensions within its purview.

More money can help, but other adjustments are also required. It would be highly desirable to explore the possibility of collapsing the time required to earn a doctorate. Some significant experiments are under way—from advanced college placement to dovetailing undergraduate and graduate programs more effectively. But two barriers stand athwart those experiments. Many educators still believe that young people should move in chronological lock step in order to assure their emotional stability. They see a danger in mixing 16- and 19-year-olds in the same college freshman class. Moreover, the American public seems to refuse to consider individuals under 21 and often even under 25 as fully responsible adults. There has been a marked tendency toward the "infantilization" of American youth which contributes to the unnecessary prolongation with corresponding excessive costs of higher education.

The current attitudes help to explain why educational and occupational guidance places so little emphasis on the expeditious completion of one's studies and the early assumption of a responsible role in the world of work. While the years of college and graduate study should be a period when the individual has an opportunity to explore and deepen his interests and competences, the protection of these important personal goals need not necessarily be in conflict with other desiderata, which include bringing one's formal education to an early successful conclusion and starting of one's career. There is ample room for a restructuring of curricula and promotion procedures and for more and better guidance aimed at the conservation of time.

There is another aspect related to the conservation of time. Many a young man, even one able to earn his doctorate expeditiously and get an early start in his career, is still likely to be plagued by financial responsibilities. Let us consider the young man who marries and is in academic life, particularly one in a field where the opportunities for outside income are relatively limited—as in the humanities. While he is in the lower ranks, his academic salary is too small to support a growing family even at a modest level. He will be strongly tempted to seek assignments which yield a little extra income. He will often turn the "free" hours that he should be devoting to further study and research into extra teaching or other routine assignments that have no value to his career other than providing him with some additional income. Much valuable talent is eroded by the struggle for existence that many face in the early years of their academic career. Since government and foundations are making ever larger sums available for research, the allocation of some part of these monies to young academicians under terms of maximum freedom to pursue their careers as *they* see fit would probably prove to be an important measure. If more young people can broaden and deepen themselves during the early years of their career, if they can assume responsibility for their own intellectual progress, it is more likely that they will prove productive.

In earlier generations relatively few people acquired a doctorate. The degree was of importance primarily to those who were set on an academic career and those who planned to practice medicine or dentistry. The last several decades have witnessed a substantial broadening of this group so that today it includes a significant proportion of those who look forward to a career in the natural or social sciences or in research in industry or government, as well as those who aspire to higher positions in many other fields such as education, business, social work, or library service.

The universities have begun to make some adjustments to these new facts of life. These include the establishing of new doctorate degrees in professional fields. But it is questionable whether they have faced the full ramifications of the vast extension that is under way. Individuals today are pursuing their education up to the doctorate, not with the aim of devoting their lives to research, but simply in order to serve in a staff or administrative capacity in profit or nonprofit organizations or in government service. Even after they have been modified, the requirements for the doctorate of philosophy do not fit the needs of most of these new professionals. And if the modification proceeds too far the new professional degree may have little in common with the essentials of a true doctorate.

This question must be faced. Soon the major universities will not be in a position to cope with the vastly enlarged numbers who will be seeking a doctorate. While the number of institutions competent to provide instruction at the doctorate level can and should be increased, this may not be sufficient to meet the increased demand—especially if standards are to be safeguarded. The range of possible alternatives should be carefully explored, including the possibility of reestablishing the importance of the master of arts and science degrees. These degrees can meet the needs of many who desire to pursue their studies beyond the baccalaureate level, but who do not necessarily have to acquire all of the competences now demanded of those who secure the doctorate.

There is scope for adjustment both upward and downward. Many who pursue the doctorate might sensibly stop short, at least initially, at the master's level while many who acquire the doctorate should look for broadened opportunities to continue their studies after they begin to work.

Although individuals with doctorates were once employed almost exclusively by the universities and the independent professions, an increasing proportion now earn their livelihood by working for large companies. Universities have long known and acted upon the principle that members of their faculties can stay abreast of progress in their own and related disciplines only if they have considerable "free" time for continuing study and research. This explains the sabbatical and particularly the nine-month academic year. However, most other employers of professional personnel do not understand the necessity for balancing routine work with opportunities for self-development. A very few corporations have introduced modifications in the time demands they make on their professional employees, but most companies continue to treat professionals as other salaried personnel. The same is true of the several levels of government and most nonprofit organizations. The outstanding exception is the Armed Forces which have long provided excellent opportunities for the further education of their personnel, especially those who have been marked for advancement.

The failure to broaden and deepen one's knowledge on a continuing basis will inevitably speed the obsolescence of what one has previously learned and mastered. It is therefore essential to the more effective utilization of talent in the United States that nonacademic employers provide adequate opportunities for the further education and training of their professional staffs. Admittedly the provision of such opportunities is difficult to arrange in a competitive environment and costly to carry out. But nothing is more costly for society as a whole than to tolerate the accelerated obsolescence that results from failure to do so.

It makes no sense to strive to find the scarce resources required to expand the universities so that they can turn out more qualified persons if a high proportion of those who graduate will be employed under conditions that insure that their skills will soon become obsolescent and that their potential will atrophy. The barriers that now block business, government, and nonprofit organizations other than universites from making adequate investments in the further education and training of their professional personnel should be carefully studied with an aim of finding effective remedies.

We cannot of course assume that all of the causes of skill obsolescence lie outside the academic realm and that all is in order in colleges and universities. There was repeated evidence in the replies we received from many of our respondents in academic life that the environment in which they found themselves exercised a deterrent influence on the further growth and development of their potential. The inadequacy of university financing was reflected in the great amount of time spent by the faculty in routine tasks that could have been better performed by others, from secretaries to research assistants, but there was no money available to hire the others. Lack of finances also resulted frequently in shortages of essential resources, from adequate libraries to adequate laboratories. Few academic institutions were able to help defray even the traveling costs which would enable many of the faculty to pursue their research away from home.

Money was not the only deficiency in the academic environment. Insensitive administrators who were more concerned with procedures and controls than the advancement of knowledge and cantankerous colleagues who found their satisfactions in in-fighting rather than in productive scholarship also detracted substantially from an optimum environment. The absence of a stimulating intellectual environment, which can be established and maintained only through the joint efforts of a sympathetic administration, congenial colleagues, and good students, probably was responsible for the greatest toll. It is hard for a man to run against his environment, especially if he has much to lose and the prospect of gain is slight. Even a man with considerable inner direction and strong work motivation will slacken his efforts to keep himself intellectually vital if he finds little support and encouragement in his environment. The location of academic institutions in out-of-the-way places was noted as a further deterrent. Lively minds need a lively environment.

It seems clear that today much intellectual potential goes to waste as a result of the many weaknesses in our institutions of higher learning. This waste is compounded because, as the faculty spends too many hours teaching or in committee work and too few on study and research, students will be less well trained and motivated. Here is a sector where major efforts at conservation are called for.

In addition to these aspects of the impact of the employment situation on the development and utilization of talent in the arena of education and training, several other facets warrant consideration. Our study showed that there was considerable mobility of highly educated persons among the different sectors of the economy—academic, corporate, nonprofit, government, and self-employment, as well as considerable mobility within the same sector. In some instances useful mobility is facilitated by an industry-wide pension and retirement system such as there is among a large number of academic institutions and among most of the agencies of the federal government. In many other instances inability to transfer pension and retirement rights undoubtedly acts as a deterrent to a man's finding the type of employment in which he can make the optimum use of his education and skills.

A more subtle but still very important deterrent to the effective utilization of specialized knowledge and skill was reported by our respondents in corporate enterprise who pointed out that the promotion and reward structures of most organizations are weighted heavily in favor of those in line management to the neglect of those who continue to pursue their specialized interests in the laboratory or in other professional work. There was repeated evidence that men who would have much preferred to pursue work within the area of their professional training but who found that they could not reach even a reasonable level of monetary reward and prestige unless they shifted into general management or sales. Although several large companies have sought to provide two routes of advancement—one for those in general management and another for those in technical work—our data suggest that these efforts so far do not provide real options for many able people. Corporate enterprise is still so structured that it pulls the abler technical people out of the fields of their specialization into general management. While this does not mean that every man with a Ph.D. in chemistry or biology who enters corporate employment should remain in the laboratory throughout his working life, the fact that many who would prefer to do so are substantially blocked from participating in the rewards that industry offers its successful employees is an impediment to the more effective utilization of talent. Further efforts to provide truly effective career opportunities for technical personnel in industry would contribute to the conservation of talent.

The hierarchical structure of industry appears to present more barriers to the effective utilization of talent than the hierarchy found in academic life. The essential difference appears to be that the scientist in industry operates largely in a closed world. His immediate circumstances and even more his future prospects are very much a function of his relationships to his superiors. If he runs into serious conflict with them, his only option is to leave and find employment elsewhere, but such a move may be very costly if he has accumulated valuable deferred benefits. An academic is in a considerably better position. A young professor can make a name outside his own institution. If his papers are published in established journals, he will soon build a reputation that his superiors must recognize; if they do not, he will have relatively little difficulty in moving to another institution. Once he has acquired tenure he can afford to go his own way, even to the extent of risking conflict with his superiors, without fear of serious reprisals. Most able academics sooner or later become largely independent of their superiors. This is not to say that the university is free of backbiting, bickering, politics, and jealousy; it states only that the constraints under which most people in the academic world operate are considerably less than those found in industry.

In corporate structure the route into middle management —and even more the route from middle into higher management—is rocky. One characteristic of this path is that most corporate supervisors tend to control the flow of ideas up and down; this makes it difficult for able young people to make their capacity known. Moreover, those who advance up the supervisory hierarchy are frequently more skillful in politics than in the technical aspects of their work, with the result that those below them frequently do not receive the professional guidance they need. Our protocols were replete with complaints about the way in which these manifestations of corporate life handicapped the development and utilization of talent. Industry faces a major challenge in this necessity to reconcile its need to control its programs, funds, and personnel with this essential task of providing competent professional leadership for its scientific and research personnel.

The foregoing difficulties are not limited to profit-making organizations. They also exist—sometimes even to an exaggerated degree, in government and nonprofit organizations. Particularly when an organization is engaged in the accomplishment of a broad program, such as the development of a new weapons system by the Armed Forces, the likelihood of serious conflicts between line and technical personnel is heightened.

Tightly structured and controlled organizations present one other important deterrent to the effective utilization of talent. Our study revealed that many of our group had broadened and deepened their competences by engaging in work-related activities off the job. But many business organizations as well as departments of government and groups in the nonprofit sector of our society do not want their personnel to engage in these activities; they are certainly disinclined to make any adjustments in time to facilitate their doing so. They try to restrict the activities of their personnel to the organization and in so doing they interfere with their continuing growth. Several of our respondents mentioned the limitations which they had experienced as a result of such organizational policies.

This brings us to the third set of relationships which we want to explore—namely, how broad public policy can better contribute to the conservation of talent. During the course of our study we noted repeatedly the many ways in which military service exercised a positive, negative, or neutral influence on the career development of our group. Most of our respondents saw service during World War II at a time when this country was engaged in a life or death struggle for survival. The war ended almost two decades ago but the draft has continued, although in recent years an ever smaller percent of the eligible age group has served in the Armed Forces. Current estimates suggest that unless there is a rapid increase in military requirements the proportion of 18-year-olds who will be required to serve will not exceed 2 out of 5. At present, students who continue to do satisfactory work in school are eligible for deferment; married men are deferred; and those who are older than 26 are not likely to be called.

There are serious defects in a Universal Military Training and Service Act which will require less than half of an age group to serve, and which promises that those who are adept enough to be deferred until they reach their 26th birthday will not have to serve. While such a loose draft system may encourage some to continue their education who otherwise might not, the social losses outweigh the benefits. Military service in a democracy is too serious a matter to justify gross inequities in selection. The present system encourages a great many young people to "play the angles" in the hope of escaping military service; moreover, it can have untoward consequences for the way in which they plan their educational and career objectives. There is a clear need for an objective system for selecting those who are required to fill the quotas and the early determination of each man's draft status (at 18 or so) so that young men can plan their future intelligently. The present uncertainty interferes unnecessarily with sound career decision making from a social as well as a personal point of view. In April, 1964, President Johnson took the first step to remedy these defects by directing the Department of Defense to undertake a comprehensive reevaluation of the draft.

The actions of young men are determined in no small measure by the actions of the young women whom they marry. During the past several decades the age at which young people marry has been dropping and so has the age at which couples start and complete their families. As we pointed out above, these developments put an added strain on the financial resources of young people, especially those who plan for an elongated period of education. The willingness of young wives to work and the willingness of parents who are in a position to do so to assist young couples has helped to ease some of these financial pressures. But many parents are in no position to help and most wives are unable to keep working after they have children.

The reasons for early marriage are easy to understand, but the forces which encourage young couples to have their children early are less evident, especially those couples who have not finished their college or graduate education. Unless there is a markedly adverse turn in employment conditions there is little prospect that the age of marriage will rise appreciably. But perhaps we can look forward to a postponement of the time when young couples start a family. The pressure for delay may come from the distaff side as women as well as their husbands recognize that they owe it to themselves not to terminate their education prematurely. Their adjustment later on, within the family and outside, will depend to a marked degree on their educational achievements.

One of the more striking findings in our study was the marked absence of discrimination perceived by the respondents during the course of their education, their military service, or their employment. Almost no one reported that he had been handicapped because of his religious or ethnic background. Since our group was intelligent and sensitive we can accept their word that discrimination played little or no part in their career development.

But there is another facet to this question that warrants consideration. Only 2 out of 342 respondents were Negroes. This very small number in an otherwise completely mixed group attests to the cumulative consequences of the centuries during which widespread racial discrimination has existed throughout American society. Negro children have frequently been forced to attend schools where the staff and facilities are grossly inadequate; the financial and other pressures under which they live are often so severe that they find it much more difficult than others to continue with advanced education; when they acquire skills and competences, they find barriers to employment.

Negroes represent about 10 percent of our population. Yet they accounted for less than one percent of the fellowship winners in our study. This is at least a rough first measure of the challenge that this country faces as it comes to grips with the eradication of all forms of racial discrimination. Political freedom for the Negro is a necessary but by no means a sufficient step to assure his full participation in American society. Three hundred and forty-five years of discriminatory treatment cannot be washed away. It will require a great many constructive actions on a great many fronts before the latent potential of the Negro population can be fully developed and utilized.

There are several other groups that are also handicapped in the further development and utilization of their talent. These include the five million Spanish-speaking people in the Northeast and the Southwest and West, and the much larger numbers of low income white families heavily concentrated in the Southeast but present in every section of the country on the farm, in small communities, and in urban centers. A great amount of valuable potential runs to waste because millions of young people are born to parents who do not have the wherewithal to give them a proper start in life, and community resources fail to provide them with an adequate range and quality of opportunities. The "war on poverty," like the "war on segregation," has been too long delayed.

While our group contained relatively few in the arts, the few who were included pointed up another shortcoming in our society. The absence of a strong demand for the work of painters, sculptors, musicians, actors, poets, and other artists means that many with talent in these fields either face a life of insecurity or even penury or must change their career objectives. Only a very few can look forward to the large rewards that are showered on the exceptional man. Artists have never been able to rely on the competitive market for their living. Yet there are relatively few institutionalized devices to assist them. The amount of money that philanthropy and government have donated to underwrite the work of artists has been very little compared to the vast sums donated toward other social ends. A society that is continually enjoying an increase in real income should give early and serious consideration to the steps it might take to provide greater incentives for the development of artistic potential and for the support of those who want to devote their lives to artistic endeavor.

Much closer to the heart of our study were the disparities we found between the support and encouragement of the natural and social sciences and that provided the humanities. The power of money is such that those in a position of authority and influence should see that the imbalances prevailing among the major fields of intellectual work are not permitted to widen further and, indeed, that efforts be made to narrow the discrepancies now existing. No society can gain in the long run from tempting men away from the type of work they are inclined to follow and where their talents lead them.

We became greatly impressed with the significant contribution that a period of sustained high level employment makes to the development and utilization of talent. A strong job market encouraged many to pursue their education to the doctorate and facilitated their or their wives' earning the necessary funds. Moreover, the strong demand for their skills meant that few were ever without work. The tight labor market gave them an opportunity to move readily from one job to another either within the same organization or in different organizations, and their mobility frequently helped them acquire additional skills. Moreover, those who found that they had made the wrong occupational choice did not face insurmountable hurdles when they contemplated a radical change. In these and still other ways the strong demand for professional, managerial, and technical personnel was a major contribution to the more effective utilization of talent.

There were, however, a few drawbacks incident to the strong market. For instance, the market encouraged excessive changing of jobs, and this had negative rather than positive results. There may have been some "spoiling" of young men by the inflated rewards which they were able to earn. But on balance the positive effects far outweighed the negative ones.

The conservation of talent truly depends upon minimum unemployment. For many young people will not develop the momentum and many will not put forth the effort required to overcome the multiple barriers that they will encounter along the preparatory route unless they see some reasonable prospects ahead. A continuing high level of employment is essential for a democratic society which has always placed and must continue to place the highest value on the freedom of the individual to choose his own career and to pursue it as he sees fit.

The solutions will not come easily, but they will come to the extent that the American people appreciate the challenge which they face and the rewards that they can gain from meeting it successfully. We dare not fail to conserve our most precious resource.

# Appendix: Questionnaire Used in Career Development Study

# ► WORK EXPERIENCE

FOR YOUR PRESENT EMPLOYMENT, complete questions 1 or 2 as applicable.

1  If self-employed, give:  Profession or business...........................Location...........................

| Date became self-employed | Annual income from business or profession First year of self-employment:   Current income: | Number of hours per week devoted to business or profession |
|---|---|---|
| Nature of your work | | |

2  If salaried, give:  Organization...................................Location...........................

| Dates<br>FROM   TO | Job title and brief description of duties | Reason for leaving previous position |
|---|---|---|
| Present | Average # hours per week devoted to job .... Present salary: | |
| FROM   TO | Previous position(s) with present employer<br><br>Average # hours per week devoted to job .... Last salary:    Starting salary: | Reason for changing position(s) |
| FROM   TO | First position with present employer<br><br>Average # hours per week devoted to job .... Last salary:    Starting salary: | Reason for leaving previous employer, if any |

3  Why did you accept employment with this organization (or start your own business)? ...........................
............................................................................................................
............................................................................................................
............................................................................................................

a.  What alternative employment were you seriously considering when you accepted your first job with this employer
(or decided to go into business for yourself)? ...........................................................
............................................................................................................

b.  How long do you expect to remain in your present position? ...............................................
............................................................................................................

c.  Under what circumstances do you think you might leave your present employer (or change your self-employed
status)? .................................................................................................
............................................................................................................
............................................................................................................
............................................................................................................
............................................................................................................

4  Work history—previous full-time or major part-time employment. Work back from present employment.

| Dates | | Employer, Location | Reason for leaving this job |
|-------|-------|-------|-------|
| FROM | TO | | |
| | | Job title & major duty<br>Average # hours per week devoted to job ....<br>Last salary:　　　Starting salary: | Reason for taking this job |
| FROM | TO | Employer, Location | Reason for leaving this job |
| | | Job title & major duty<br>Average # hours per week devoted to job ....<br>Last salary:　　　Starting salary: | Reason for taking this job |
| FROM | TO | Employer, Location | Reason for leaving this job |
| | | Job title & major duty<br>Average # hours per week devoted to job ....<br>Last salary:　　　Starting salary: | Reason for taking this job |
| FROM | TO | Employer, Location | Reason for leaving this job |
| | | Job title & major duty<br>Average # hours per week devoted to job ....<br>Last salary:　　　Starting salary: | Reason for taking this job |
| FROM | TO | Employer, Location | Reason for leaving this job |
| | | Job title & major duty<br>Average # hours per week devoted to job ....<br>Last salary:　　　Starting salary: | Reason for taking this job |
| FROM | TO | Employer, Location | Reason for leaving this job |
| | | Job title & major duty<br>Average # hours per week devoted to job ....<br>Last salary:　　　Starting salary: | Reason for taking this job |
| FROM | TO | Employer, Location | Reason for leaving this job |
| | | Job title & major duty<br>Average # hours per week devoted to job ....<br>Last salary:　　　Starting salary: | Reason for taking this job |
| FROM | TO | Employer, Location | Reason for leaving this job |
| | | Job title & major duty<br>Average # hours per week devoted to job ....<br>Last salary:　　　Starting salary: | Reason for taking this job |

*If more space is required, please continue on the additional page at the end of this questionnaire using this general format.*

5 Please explain any period during which you were not working, other than time in school or military service.

........................................................................................................................

........................................................................................................................

........................................................................................................................

........................................................................................................................

a. *If you are not now working, do you expect to work again, either part- or full-time?*   Yes (  )   No (  )

b. *If so, when?* ...........................*at what kind of work?* ............................................

........................................................................................................................

c. *If not, why not?* ..............................................................................................

........................................................................................................................

6 In light of your present major interests in work, which of your jobs have significantly:

a. *Contributed to your occupational development? How?* ......................................................

........................................................................................................................

........................................................................................................................

b. *Interfered with it? How?* ....................................................................................

........................................................................................................................

........................................................................................................................

7 In connection with any phase of your employment, did you receive *specific* training or gain *special* experience, over and above that normally secured on that type of job, which you feel has definitely contributed to your career so far or which you expect to prove to be a significant asset in the future?   Yes (  )   No (  )

a. *If so, briefly describe how the training or experience contributed to your career* .......................

........................................................................................................................

........................................................................................................................

........................................................................................................................

8 As you look back over your working life, can you identify any persons who played a *key* role in your career, particularly with respect to influencing the nature or direction of your work?   Yes (  )   No (  )

a. *If so, in what relationship did they stand to you, and in what way did they affect your career?* ...................

........................................................................................................................

........................................................................................................................

........................................................................................................................

9 With regard to your full-time employment    continued in the same line of work?   (  )
to date, do you feel that you have:    shifted your emphasis within the same general area of work?   (  )
changed your line of work substantially?   (  )

a. *If you have shifted emphasis or changed substantially, what considerations prompted your action?* ................

........................................................................................................................

........................................................................................................................

........................................................................................................................

10　Did you ever seriously consider changing from one kind of work to another but decide not to?　Yes (　)　No (　)

　　a. *If so, into what area of work did you plan to move?* ...........................................................

　　...................................................................................................................

　　...................................................................................................................

　　b. *What prompted you not to do so?* ...........................................................................

　　...................................................................................................................

　　...................................................................................................................

　　...................................................................................................................

11　With respect to your area of work, do you　continue in the same line of work?　(　)
　　think that during the next decade you will:　shift your emphasis within the same general area of work?　(　)
　　　　　　　　　　　　　　　　　　　　　change your line of work substantially?　(　)

　　a. *If you anticipate shifting emphasis or changing, into which area of work are you likely to move, and why?*

　　...................................................................................................................

　　...................................................................................................................

　　...................................................................................................................

　　...................................................................................................................

12　With respect to your own progress, do you anticipate that over the next decade you will:

　　　　have about the same responsibilities and duties as you now have?　(　)
　　　　be doing somewhat more significant work with some increase in recognition and rewards?　(　)
　　　　experience substantial growth in your career with concomitant recognition and rewards?　(　)

　　a. *What do you expect to be the next step in your advancement, and when do you expect it to occur?* .............

　　...................................................................................................................

　　...................................................................................................................

　　...................................................................................................................

13　On balance, do you feel that in terms of your earlier expectations your present work provides the satisfactions and
　　rewards which you had expected by this time?　Yes (　)　No (　)

　　a. *If not, do some aspects of your work fall short of expectations?*　Yes (　)　No (　)　*If so, which?* ........

　　...................................................................................................................

　　...................................................................................................................

　　...................................................................................................................

　　b. *Or, do some aspects of your work exceed expectations?*　Yes (　)　No (　)　*If so, which?* .............

　　...................................................................................................................

　　...................................................................................................................

　　...................................................................................................................

14　What do you consider to be the most gratifying aspects of your present work? ....................................

　　...................................................................................................................

　　...................................................................................................................

　　a. *The least gratifying?* .......................................................................................

　　...................................................................................................................

► ADDITIONAL ACTIVITIES

15 Please complete the pertinent sections below for those activities in which you have engaged, either in addition to your regular job or between the periods of employment noted in the previous section. In describing the nature of the activity, please indicate the role you played.

A. GOVERNMENT SERVICE, including consulting work, advisory committees, reserve duty, etc.

   a. Have you ever engaged in this type of activity?    Yes ( )    No ( )    If so, when? ...................

   b. Nature of activity ................................................................................................
   ....................................................................................................................
   ....................................................................................................................

   c. Average time spent:    a few hours per month    ( )    at least a day a week    ( )
      (check one)            a few hours per week     ( )    2 or more days a week    ( )

   d. Why undertaken:     as civic, religious or social obligation    ( )
      (if several          to further professional development    ( )
      apply, number        as change from main work activity    ( )
      in order of          for supplementary income    ( )
      importance)          for enjoyment    ( )
                           other (health, prestige, etc.) .........................    ( )

B. NON-GOVERNMENTAL: free-lance activities; consulting work; independent research; part-time employment.

   a. Have you ever engaged in this type of activity?    Yes ( )    No ( )    If so, when? ...................

   b. Nature of activity ................................................................................................
   ....................................................................................................................
   ....................................................................................................................

   c. Average time spent:    a few hours per month    ( )    at least a day a week    ( )
      (check one)            a few hours per week     ( )    2 or more days a week    ( )

   d. Why undertaken:     as civic, religious or social obligation    ( )
      (if several          to further professional development    ( )
      apply, number        as change from main work activity    ( )
      in order of          for supplementary income    ( )
      importance)          for enjoyment    ( )
                           other (health, prestige, etc.) .........................    ( )

C. PROFESSIONAL SOCIETIES; business or professional associations.

   a. Have you ever engaged in this type of activity?    Yes ( )    No ( )    If so, when? ...................

   b. Nature of activity ................................................................................................
   ....................................................................................................................
   ....................................................................................................................

   c. Average time spent:    a few hours per month    ( )    at least a day a week    ( )
      (check one)            a few hours per week     ( )    2 or more days a week    ( )

   d. Why undertaken:     as civic, religious or social obligation    ( )
      (if several          to further professional development    ( )
      apply, number        as change from main work activity    ( )
      in order of          for supplementary income    ( )
      importance)          for enjoyment    ( )
                           other (health, prestige, etc.) .........................    ( )

ADDITIONAL ACTIVITIES
15 *(Continued)*

D.  CIVIC, POLITICAL OR SCHOOL ACTIVITIES; fraternal or service clubs; religious groups.

   *a.  Have you ever engaged in this type of activity?*  Yes ( )  No ( )  *If so, when?* ....................

   *b.  Nature of activity* ...........................................................................................

   ...........................................................................................................

   ...........................................................................................................

   *c.  Average time spent:*  *a few hours per month* ( )  *at least a day a week* ( )
     *(check one)*       *a few hours per week* ( )  *2 or more days a week* ( )

   *d.  Why undertaken:*  *as civic, religious or social obligation* ( )
     *(if several*     *to further professional development* ( )
     *apply, number*   *as change from main work activity* ( )
     *in order of*     *for supplementary income* ( )
     *importance)*     *for enjoyment* ( )
                  *other (health, prestige, etc.)* ......................... ( )

E.  HOBBIES OR OTHER LEISURE-TIME ACTIVITIES.

   *a.  Have you ever engaged in this type of activity?*  Yes ( )  No ( )  *If so, when?* ..................

   *b.  Nature of activity* ...........................................................................................

   ...........................................................................................................

   ...........................................................................................................

   *c.  Average time spent:*  *a few hours per month* ( )  *at least a day a week* ( )
     *(check one)*       *a few hours per week* ( )  *2 or more days a week* ( )

   *d.  Why undertaken:*  *as civic, religious or social obligation* ( )
     *(if several*     *to further professional development* ( )
     *apply, number*   *as change from main work activity* ( )
     *in order of*     *for supplementary income* ( )
     *importance)*     *for enjoyment* ( )
                  *other (health, prestige, etc.)* ......................... ( )

16 Has your participation in any of these activities contributed to your career development?  Yes ( )  No ( )

   *a.  If so, please explain* ......................................................................................

   ...........................................................................................................

   ...........................................................................................................

   ...........................................................................................................

17 Has your participation in any of these activities interfered in any way with your career development?  Yes (
                                                                       No (

   *a.  If so, please explain* ......................................................................................

   ...........................................................................................................

   ...........................................................................................................

   ...........................................................................................................

18  Did you have a definite occupational
    goal in mind:                                    Yes        No                    If so, what was it?

    Upon entering college?                           ( )        ( )       ......................................................

    Upon completing college?                         ( )        ( )       ......................................................

    During your graduate studies?                    ( )        ( )       ......................................................

    Upon completing graduate study?                  ( )        ( )       ......................................................

19  Did any of the following factors significantly aid or hinder your pursuit of *graduate* studies?

| | aided | hindered | | aided | hindered |
|---|---|---|---|---|---|
| Family background | ( ) | ( ) | Graduate scholarship or fellowship | ( ) | ( ) |
| Undergraduate preparation | ( ) | ( ) | Extra-curricular activities | ( ) | ( ) |
| Financial resources | ( ) | ( ) | Military service or experience | ( ) | ( ) |
| Working, either part- or full-time | ( ) | ( ) | Educational benefits of GI Bill | ( ) | ( ) |
| Marriage and/or other family responsibilities | ( ) | ( ) | Other: ......................... ( ) | ( ) |

    a.  If any of these factors had a pronounced effect, please explain ......................................
    ...................................................................................................
    ...................................................................................................

20  What employment, in addition to that which you have noted in question 4 above, did you engage in during your years
    of *graduate study?* ................................................................................
    ...................................................................................................

    a.  If you worked, how did it affect your occupational choice or otherwise influence your career? ...................
    ...................................................................................................
    ...................................................................................................

21  What university or other formal education or training did you undertake *after* leaving Columbia University?

| INSTITUTION | FIELD OF STUDY | DATES | DEGREES, IF ANY, AND DATE THEREOF |
|---|---|---|---|
| ................................... | ................................ | ............... | ............................... |
| ................................... | ................................ | ............... | ............................... |
| ................................... | ................................ | ............... | ............................... |

22  If you had such additional education or training, please briefly explain:

    a.  Reasons for undertaking it ....................................................................
    ...................................................................................................
    ...................................................................................................

    b.  Its relation to your subsequent work experience .................................................
    ...................................................................................................
    ...................................................................................................

23  Do you feel that your formal education was adequate in preparing you for your work?     Yes ( )     No ( )

    a.  If not, please explain .........................................................................
    ...................................................................................................
    ...................................................................................................

► MILITARY OR CIVILIAN WAR SERVICE

24 Have you had active military service?    *Yes* (  )    *No* (  )    If so, give dates............................

and Service ............................................................................................................

   *a.  What was your rank or grade at entry?* ............................*at separation?* ..........................

   *b.  Briefly describe the nature of your duty* ....................................................................

............................................................................................................

   *c.  What influence, if any, did your experience on active military service have upon your occupational choice or your career development?*

............................................................................................................

............................................................................................................

25 Were you engaged in defense or related civilian work or in government service during either World War II or the Korean conflict?    *Yes* (  )    *No* (  )

   *a.  If so, give dates and briefly describe* ......................................................................

............................................................................................................

............................................................................................................

   *b.  In the absence of the war situation would you have undertaken this kind of work?*    *Yes* (  )    *No* (  )

   *c.  What influence, if any, did this work experience have upon your occupational choice or subsequent career?*

............................................................................................................

............................................................................................................

26 Aside from any influence which your specific wartime experience may have had, did the involvement of the United States in these major conflicts and their aftermath directly or indirectly affect your choice of occupation or otherwise influence your career development?    *Yes* (  )    *No* (  )

   *a.  If so, in what way?* ........................................................................................

............................................................................................................

............................................................................................................

............................................................................................................

► FAMILY AND MARRIAGE

27 Where was your father born? ......................................your mother? ..........................

28 What was your father's occupation? ................................................................................

   *a.  Was your father working in this occupation during your college years?*    *Yes* (  )    *No* (  )

   *If not, please give the date of his retirement* ..........................*or death* ..........................

   *b.  Did your mother work after her marriage?*    *Yes* (  )    *No* (  )

   *If so, what did she do?* ......................................................................................

   *c.  In what way, if any, did either parent's work or life circumstances (severe illness, death, etc.) affect your career?*

............................................................................................................

............................................................................................................

............................................................................................................

............................................................................................................

29 Have you ever married?     *Yes* (  )     *No* (  )     If so, when? .............................................

   *a. Number of children* .....................*Year each born* .....................................

   *b. In what way did marriage or having children affect your career?* ......................................

   .............................................................................................................

   .............................................................................................................

30 Was your marriage broken by death (  ), divorce (  ), or separation (  )? If so, when? ..........................

   *a. If so, what effect did this have on your work or career?* ...........................................

   .............................................................................................................

   .............................................................................................................

   *b. Have you remarried?*     *Yes* (  )     *No* (  )     *When?* ..................................................

31 Has your spouse worked?     *Yes* (  )     *No* (  )

   *a. If so, when?* ....................*and at what kind of work?* .............................................

   *b. Has her (or his) work or career affected your own career in any way?*     *Yes* (  )     *No* (  )

   *c. If so, how?* ...........................................................................................

   .............................................................................................................

   .............................................................................................................

32 Were any *decisions* which you made about choice of occupation, selection of a particular job, remaining in or shifting your line of work affected by any other family considerations (wife, children, parents)?     *Yes* (  )     *No* (  )

   *a. If so, in what way?* ...................................................................................

   .............................................................................................................

   .............................................................................................................

   .............................................................................................................

▶  GENERAL

33 Have special factors (such as prizes or honors, degrees, publications or other original productions, personal illness, etc.), either by their presence or absence, significantly influenced your career?     *Yes* (  )     *No* (  )

   *a. If so, please explain* ................................................................................

   .............................................................................................................

   .............................................................................................................

   .............................................................................................................

34 Have the time and energy which you have devoted to your work changed over the past decade owing to changes in the nature of your work, family responsibilities, or personal considerations?     *Yes* (  )     *No* (  )

   *a. If so, briefly explain* ...............................................................................

   .............................................................................................................

   .............................................................................................................

   .............................................................................................................

35  In retrospect, were there attractive career choices or opportunities that you did not pursue?    *Yes* ( )    *No* ( )

a.  *If so, what were they?* ...................................................................................................

..............................................................................................................................

..............................................................................................................................

b.  *Why did you not pursue them?* .......................................................................................

..............................................................................................................................

..............................................................................................................................

c.  *Any regrets?* ..............................................................................................................

..............................................................................................................................

36  On balance, as you have reviewed your career, what strikes you as the *major factors* that have, on one hand, contributed to and, on the other, definitely interfered with your currently working at the level you believe to be commensurate with your abilities and interests? *Please list below in order of importance.*

| CONTRIBUTING | INTERFERING |
|---|---|
| (1) .................................................. | (1) .................................................. |
| (2) .................................................. | (2) .................................................. |
| (3) .................................................. | (3) .................................................. |

37  What do you expect that you will be doing:

a.  *10 years from now?* ....................................................................................................

b.  *20 years from now?* ....................................................................................................

c.  *According to your present plans, when do you expect to retire?* ...........................................

d.  *What do you expect to do after retirement?* ...................................................................

..............................................................................................................................

..............................................................................................................................

38  Will you please elaborate or clarify any of your above answers if you feel that it would be helpful to us and, in addition, comment upon any other points that you consider important in connection with your work and career? Please use the additional pages if necessary.

..............................................................................................................................

..............................................................................................................................

..............................................................................................................................

..............................................................................................................................

..............................................................................................................................

..............................................................................................................................

..............................................................................................................................

..............................................................................................................................

..............................................................................................................................

..............................................................................................................................

# Bibliography

Allport, G. W. *Personality: A Psychological Interpretation.* New York, Holt, 1937.

Allport, G. W., P. W. Vernon, and G. Lindzey. *Study of Values.* Boston, Manual of Directions, 1951.

Aydelotte, Frank. *The American Rhodes Scholarships: A Review of the First Forty Years.* Princeton, Princeton University Press, 1946.

Barelson, Bernard. *Graduate Education in the United States.* New York, McGraw-Hill, 1960.

Barow, Henry. *Men in a World at Work.* Boston, Houghton Mifflin, 1964.

Barron, Frank X. *Creativity and Psychological Health.* Princeton, Van Nostrand, 1963.

Becker, Howard S. and J. W. Carper. "Development of Identification with an Occupation," *American Sociological Review,* 61 (January 1956), 289-98.

—— "Elements of Identification with an Occupation," *American Sociological Review,* 21 (June 1956), 341-48.

Bray, Douglas W. *Issues in the Study of Talent.* New York, King's Crown Press, 1954.

Brayfield, A. H. and W. H. Crockett. "Employee Attitudes and Employee Performance," *Psychological Bulletin,* Vol. 52, No. 5 (1955), pp. 396-424.

Brinton, Crane, ed. *The Society of Fellows.* Cambridge, Harvard University Press, 1959.

Bühler, Charlotte. *Der Menschliche Lebenslauf als Psychologisches Problem.* Leipzig, Verlag Von S. Hirzel, 1933.

Caplow, T. and R. McGee. *The Academic Marketplace.* New York, Basic Books, 1954.

Clark, Kenneth E. *America's Psychologists.* Washington, D.C., American Psychological Association, 1957.

Davis, J. W. "Great Aspirations: Career Plans of America's June, 1961, College Graduates," Chicago, NORC, mimeo, 1961.

Flanagan, John C. *Design for a Study of American Youth.* Boston, Houghton Mifflin, 1962.

Flanagan, John C. et al. *Project Talent: A Survey and Follow up Study of Educational Plans.* Pittsburgh, University of Pittsburgh Press, 1962.

Fredrickson, Norman and W. B. Schraider. "Adjustment to College: A Study of 10,000 Veteran and Non-Veteran Students in Sixteen American Colleges." Princeton, Educational Testing Service, 1951.

Gardner, John W. *Excellence.* New York, Harper, 1961.

—— *Self-Renewal: The Individual and the Innovative Society.* New York, Harper and Row, 1964.

Getzels, Jacob W. and Phillip W. Jackson. *Creativity and Intelligence.* New York, Wiley, 1962.

Ginsburg, Sol W. *A Psychiatrist's Views on Social Issues.* New York, Columbia University Press, 1963.

Ginzberg, Eli. *Human Resources.* New York, Simon and Schuster, 1958.

—— "Perspectives in Work Motivation," *Personnel* (July 1954).

Ginzberg, Eli et al. *Patterns of Performance.* Vol. 3 of *The Ineffective Soldier.* New York, Columbia University Press, 1959.

Ginzberg, Eli, Sol W. Ginsburg, Sidney Axelrad, and John L. Herma. *Occupational Choice.* New York, Columbia University Press, 1951.

Herzberg, Frederick, Bernard Mausner, and Barbara B. Snyderman. *The Motivation to Work.* New York, Wiley, 1959.

Hughes, E. C. *Men and Their Work.* Glencoe, Ill., Free Press, 1958.

—— "Personality Types and the Division of Labor," *American Journal of Sociology*, 33 (1928), 754-69.

Inkeles, Alex. "Industrial Man: The Relations of Status to

Experience, Perception and Value," *The American Journal of Sociology*, Vol. LXVI, No. 1 (July 1960).

Kagan, Jerome and Howard A. Moss. *Birth to Maturity*. New York, Wiley, 1962.

Kappel, Frederick. "From the World of College to the World of Work" (J. F. Green Lecture, Westminster College), *Bell Telephone Magazine* (Spring 1962).

Keller, Suzanne. *Beyond the Ruling Class*. New York, Random House, 1963.

Kilpatrick, Franklin P. *The Image of the Federal Service*. Washington, D.C., Brookings Institution, 1964.

Kluckhohn, Clyde and others. "Values and Value: Orientations in the Theory of Action," in Talcott Parsons and Edward Shils, eds., *Toward a General Theory of Action*. Cambridge, Harvard University Press, 1951.

Kluckhohn, Florence, Fred L. Strodbeck et al. *Variations in Value Orientations*. Evanston, Ill., Row Peterson, 1961.

Knapp, Robert H. and H. B. Goodrich. *Origins of American Scientists*. Chicago, University of Chicago Press, 1952.

Knapp, Robert H. and Joseph J. Greenbaum. *The Younger American Scholar: His Collegiate Origins*. Chicago, University of Chicago Press, 1953.

Lehman, Harvey C. *Age and Achievement*. Princeton, Princeton University Press, 1953.

Lewin, Kurt. "The Psychology of Success and Failure," *Occupation*, XIV (1936), 926-30.

McClelland, David C. *Studies in Motivation*. New York, Appleton-Century-Crofts, 1955.

McClelland, David C. et al. *The Achievement Motive*. New York, Appleton-Century-Crofts, 1953.

MacKinnon, Donald W. "The Nature and Nurture of Creative Talent," *American Psychologist*, Vol. XVII, No. 7 (July 1962), pp. 484-95.

Marcson, Simon. *The Scientist in American Industry*. Princeton University, Industrial Relations Section, 1960.

Maslow, A. H. *Motivation and Personality*. New York, Harper, 1954.

Murray, H. A. *Explorations in Personality*. New York and London, Oxford University Press, 1938.

National Research Council. *Doctorate Production in United States Universities, 1920-1962*. National Academy of Sciences, Publ. 1142, 1962.

National Science Foundation. *American Science Manpower, 1956-58*. A Report of the National Register of Scientific and Technical Personnel, NSF 61-45, 1961.

—— *American Science Manpower, 1960*. A Report of the National Register of Scientific and Technical Personnel, NSF 62-43, 1962.

—— *Two Years after the College Degree: Work and Further Study Patterns*. Washington, D.C., Bureau of Sociological Research, 1963.

Newcomer, Mabel. *The Big Business Executive*. New York, Columbia University Press, 1955.

Nosow, Sigmund and W. H. Form, eds. *Man, Work and Society: A Reader in the Sociology of Occupations*. New York, Basic Books, 1962.

Riesman, David. *The Lonely Crowd: A Study of the Changing American Character*. New Haven, Yale University Press, 1950.

Roe, Anne. *The Making of a Scientist*. New York, Dodd, Mead, 1953.

—— *The Psychology of Occupations*. New York, Wiley, 1956.

Rosenberg, Morris, with the assistance of E. A. Suchman and Rose K. Goldsen. *Occupations and Values*. Glencoe, Ill., Free Press, 1957.

Rosenhaupt, Hans, with the assistance of Thomas J. Chinlund. *Graduate Students Experience at Columbia University, 1940-56*. New York, Columbia University Press, 1958.

Super, Donald E. *The Psychology of Careers*. New York, Harper, 1957.

Super, Donald E. et al. *Vocational Development: A Framework for Research*. New York, Bureau of Publications, Teachers College, Columbia University, 1957.

Taylor, Calvin and Frank Barron. *Scientific Creativity: Its Recognition and Development.* New York, Wiley, 1963.

Terman, Lewis M. and Melita H. Oden. *Genetic Studies of Genius. Vol. V: The Gifted Group at Mid-Life.* Stanford, Stanford University Press, 1959.

Tiedeman, D. V., R. P. O'Hara, and R. W. Baruch. *Career Development, Choice and Adjustment.* Princeton CEEB, 1963.

Walters, Roy W., Jr. and Douglas W. Bray. "Today's Search for Tomorrow's Leaders," *Journal of College Placement* (October 1963), pp. 22-116.

Warner, W. Lloyd and J. C. Abegglen. *Big Business Leaders in America.* New York, Harper, 1955.

White, Robert W. *Lives in Progress: A Study of the Natural Growth of Personality.* New York, Dryden, 1952.

Williams, Robin, Jr. *American Society: A Sociological Interpretation.* New York, Knopf, 1960.

Wilson, Logan. *The Academic Man: A Study in the Sociology of a Profession.* New York, Oxford University Press, 1942.

Wolfle, Dael. *America's Resources of Specialized Talent.* Report of the Commission on Human Resources and Advanced Training. New York, Harper, 1954.

Znaniecki, Florian. *The Social Role of the Man of Knowledge.* New York, Columbia University Press, 1940.

# The Conservation of
# Human Resources Project

The Conservation of Human Resources Project was established by General Dwight D. Eisenhower at Columbia University in 1950 to undertake basic research in human resources. It has been supported by grants from corporations, foundations, and the federal government. Dr. Lawrence H. Chamberlain, the Vice President of the University, exercises administrative supervision over the project.

The following bibliography includes the publications of the Conservation of Human Resources Project. It also includes several books by the director and his associates which were published prior to the formal establishment of the project but which are an integral part of the more than two decades of basic research on human resources undertaken by this interdisciplinary group at Columbia University. All books have been published by Columbia University Press, except those for which other publishers are indicated.

Bray, Douglas W. *Issues in the Study of Talent.* 1954.
Committee on the Function of Nursing, Eli Ginzberg, chairman. *A Program for the Nursing Profession.* New York, Macmillan, 1948.
Ginsburg, Sol W. *A Psychiatrist's Views on Social Issues,* 1963.
Ginzberg, Eli. *Grass on the Slag Heaps: The Story of the Welsh Miners.* New York, Harper, 1942.
—— *Human Resources: The Wealth of a Nation.* New York, Simon and Schuster, 1958.
—— *The Labor Leader.* New York, Macmillan, 1948.
—— *A Pattern for Hospital Care.* 1949.

Ginzberg, Eli. *Report on Manpower Utilization in Israel.* Jerusalem, Prime Minister's Office, 1961.

Ginzberg, Eli and associates. *The Unemployed.* New York, Harper, 1943.

Ginzberg, Eli et al. *The Ineffective Soldier: Lessons for Management and the Nation.* 1959.

Vol. 1: *The Lost Divisions.* With James K. Anderson, Sol W. Ginsburg, and John L. Herma.

Vol. 2: *Breakdown and Recovery.* With James K. Anderson, Sol W. Ginsburg, John L. Herma, and John B. Miner.

Vol. 3: *Patterns of Performance.* With James K. Anderson, Douglas W. Bray, Sol W. Ginsburg, John L. Herma, William A. Jordan, and Francis J. Ryan.

Ginzberg, Eli, assisted by James K. Anderson, Douglas W. Bray, and Robert W. Smuts. *The Negro Potential.* 1956.

Ginzberg, Eli, James K. Anderson, and John L. Herma. *The Optimistic Tradition and American Youth.* 1962.

Ginzberg, Eli, Sol W. Ginsburg, Sidney Axelrad, and John L. Herma. *Occupational Choice: An Approach to a General Theory.* 1951.

Ginzberg, Eli and Ivar E. Berg, with John L. Herma and James K. Anderson. *Democratic Values and The Rights of Management.* 1963.

Ginzberg, Eli and Hyman Berman. *The American Worker in the Twentieth Century: A History Through Autobiographies.* New York, Free Press of Glencoe, Macmillan, 1963.

Ginzberg, Eli and Douglas W. Bray. *The Uneducated.* 1953.

Ginzberg, Eli and Alfred S. Eichner. *The Troublesome Presence: American Democracy and the Negro,* New York, Free Press of Glencoe, Macmillan, 1964.

Ginzberg, Eli, Sol W. Ginsburg, and John L. Herma. *Psychiatry and Military Manpower Policy: A Reappraisal of the Experience in World War II.* 1953.

Ginzberg, Eli and Ewing W. Reilley. *Effecting Change in Large Organizations.* 1957.

Ginzberg, Eli and Peter Rogatz. *Planning for Better Hospital Care.* 1961.
Ginzberg, Eli, ed. *The Nation's Children.* 1960.
  Vol. 1: *The Family and Social Change.*
  Vol. 2: *Development and Education.*
  Vol. 3: *Problems and Prospects.*
—— *Technology and Social Change.* 1964.
—— *Values and Ideals of American Youth.* 1961.
Ginzberg, Eli, chairman. *What Makes an Executive: Report of a Round Table on Executive Potential and Performance.* 1955.
Hiestand, Dale L. *Economic Growth and Employment Opportunities for Minorities.* 1964.
Smuts, Robert W. *European Impressions of the American Worker.* 1953.
—— *Women and Work in America.* 1959.

Members of the Conservation of Human Resources Project staff have contributed to the following books of the National Manpower Council at Columbia University, all published by Columbia University Press:

*Education and Manpower.* Henry David, ed. 1960.
*Improving the Work Skills of the Nation.* 1955.
*A Policy for Scientific and Professional Manpower.* 1953.
*A Policy for Skilled Manpower.* 1954.
*Proceedings of a Conference on the Utilization of Scientific and Professional Manpower.* 1954.
*Student Deferment and National Manpower Policy.* 1952.
*Womanpower.* 1957.
*Work in the Lives of Married Women.* 1958.

# Index

Abegglen, J. C., 4
Academic setting, 27-28, 84-85, 93; and work satisfactions, 149
Achievement level, 8, 9, 90-93, 100, 103, 106, 109, 111, 202, 205; examples, 93-95; and income, 95-96; age, 96-97, 98; doctorate, 97-98, 103-4, 207; family background, 99-101; undergraduate, 101-2; grades, 102-3, 111, 205; military service, 104-6, 205, 207; first job, 106; field and function, 107-9; job mobility, 109-10; career pattern, 110-11; value orientations, 135-36; work satisfactions, 151, 164-65, 172; marriage and children, 180, 181, 182, 187, 205, 207; and activities, 192-93; and retirement, 195-96; and social reality, 206-9; and response mechanisms, 211-14
Activities, 9, 188-94, 213
Administration (function), 84, 108, 148
Age of respondents, 26; at occupational choice, 51-52; at college graduation, 54; at marriage, 58-59, 179-81; at birth of first child, 59-60, 181-82; at first job, 60, 106; at doctorate, 81, 97-98; and achievement level, 96-98; expect to retire, 194-95
Arts, the, 91, 222-23, 236-37; those in, 207-8

Barron, Frank, 5-6
Birthplace, 34-36, 38-39, 99
Broad career pattern, 70-72, 74-76, 80-87, 118, 134-35, 150, 156-57, 163, 179, 186, 195-96, 212
Broken home, effect of, 35, 38, 39-40, 41

Business, 83, 107, 147; studies of success in, 4; see also Corporate enterprise

Career: development, 8-10, 200-5; conflict over, 41-42; alternatives, see Shift; see also Career patterns
Career patterns, 9, 68-69, 88; and job mobility, 66-67, 85-86; and direction and continuity, 67-68, 71, 155; kinds of, 69-72; and occupational choice, 80, 81; and grades, 80-81; and doctorate, 81, 155; and military service, 82; and field, 82-84; and function, 84; and setting, 84-85; and personality characteristics, 86-88; and achievement level, 110-11; and value orientations, 134-35; and work satisfactions and expectations, 150, 152, 163; and goals, 155, 156-57; and marriage and children, 179, 181, 182, 186-87; and activities, 193; and retirement, 195-96; and response mechanisms, 212-13
Carnegie Corporation, 16
Children: number of, per respondent, 30, 182; effect of, 59-60, 181-83, 184-88
Clark, Kenneth, 92-93
Classics (respondents), 28-29, 32, 39-40, 74
Columbia College, 30-31, 101
Columbia University, 14-15
Community activities, 190-91; see also Activities
Concomitants, 140, 142-52, 160-62, 163
Conditions of work, 141, 143, 144, 161, 162, 165
Conservation of Human Resources Project, 6-7, 257

Continuity, in career development, 67-68, 71, 79-80, 216-17; *see also* Direction

Corporate enterprise, 28; and career pattern, 84-85; and achievement level, 93, 109; and value orientation, 129-30; and work satisfactions, 149; and further development, 227, 230-31

Death of father, 35, 39-40, 41
Depression, effect of, 39, 41-42
Deterrents, to career, 207-8; finances, 42; interruptions, 67-68, 156; marriage as, 184-88; activities as, 192; setting, 228-33
Direction, in career, 67, 71, 155; *see also* Continuity
Discrimination, 100, 235-36
Divorce, 40
Doctorate, 30, 212, 225-27; acquisition of, 54-56, 60, 64, 81-82, 103-4, 223; and achievement level, 97-98, 103-4, 207; study beyond, 227-28

Education: background of group, 30-31, 63-64; role of, in career development, 31-32, 53-54, 72, 101, 202-3, 207; financing of, 221-24; *see also* Doctorate
Emotional stability, 201
Employers, influence of, 52
Engineering (field), 27, 51, 83-84, 107, 147
Engineering (respondents), 23, 75-76, 94, 140
English (respondents), 32, 62, 125-26; and work satisfactions, 140, 143-44, 160, 161; and future, 171, 195
Environment (work), 143, 144, 227-29; *see also* Setting
Expectations, 158-59, 162-63, 165-67; and intrinsic aspects, 159-60, 163; and extrinsic aspects, 160-62, 163; and career pattern, 163; and achievement level, 164-65; and value orientation, 164-65; *see also* Future; Work satisfactions

Extrinsic aspects of work, 140, 142-52, 160-62, 163, 164-65; *see also* Income; Rewards; Status

Family: parental, 34-42, 99-101, 106; marital, 58-60, 62, 64-65, 178-88, 210
Fellowships, 44
Field (occupational), 27, 50-51, 83-84, 91, 107, 135, 146-47, 152-53, 156-57, 214
Finances: and education, 42-44, 221-24; and early career, 225
First job, 60-63, 65
Foreign born, 34-35, 36, 99
Freedom (work satisfaction), 139-40, 142, 144-45, 147-52, 159
Free-time, impingement on, 197-98; *see also* Activities
Function, in occupational field, 27, 84, 97, 108-11, 146, 148-49, 152-53, 163, 214
Future, plans for, 167-70, 172, 173-76; *see also* Retirement

GI Bill, 33, 34, 42, 222
Goals, 113, 156-58, 174-76, 214-15; *see also* Expectations; Future
Government (occupational field), 28, 149, 189-90, 227, 229-30; and achievement level, 93-94
Government (respondents), 19, 73, 76, 123, 142, 195
Grades: and career pattern, 80-81; and achievement level, 102-3, 106, 205
Grinnell College, 31

High School, importance of, 32
Hobbies, 189, 191-92; *see also* Activities
Honors, undergraduate, 101-2
Humanities, 27, 83, 91, 107, 146-47, 237
Ideological type, 120-21, 126-27, 129, 130-31, 133-35, 211; and work satisfactions, 152, 165; and marital family, 180-82, 187-88
Illness, effect of, 40, 61, 208

Income, 28-29, 44, 91, 130, 146, 150, 153, 163; other than salary, 28-29, 189-90; and achievement level, 91, 93-96; and work satisfactions, 140, 142-43, 145, 160-61, 165

Individualistic type, 117-18, 122-23, 128-29, 133-36, 196; and work satisfactions, 151-52, 165; and marital family, 180, 182, 187-88

Influence, of key persons, 52-54, 65, 174, 176

Institute of Personality Assessment and Research (Calif.), 5-6

Institutional setting, see Setting; see also Academic setting; Corporate enterprise; Government; Nonprofit organizations; Self-employed

Intermediate achievement level, 93-96, 98-100, 103-9, 110, 135, 151, 164, 180, 187; see also Achievement level

Interpersonal relations, 196, 229, 231; as work satisfaction, 140, 143-45, 146, 161

Interruption of career, 67-68, 97, 156; see also Military service

Intrinsic aspects of work, 139-42, 144-53, 159-60, 162-63

Investment (response mechanism), 210-11, 214

Ivy League colleges, 30, 31-32, 101

Job, first, 60-63, 65

Johnson, Lyndon B., 234

Journalism (respondents), 31-32, 39, 77, 95, 140, 143, 161, 183, 193

Korean War, 33

Krout, John A., 15-16

Languages (respondents), 32, 36, 37-38, 42, 144, 161, 193, 195

Law (respondents), 18, 19, 73, 124, 140, 141, 159, 161, 162, 183, 185

Leadership type, 118-19, 123-24, 129-30, 133-36; and work satisfactions, 152, 164-65

Leisure, 191-92, 193, 194; see also Activities

Liberal arts, 31-32; see also Humanities

Librarians (respondents), 43, 61, 171-72

Lower achievement level, 94-105, 107-11, 135-36, 151, 164, 180-82, 187, 193, 195, 213

Luck, 22-23, 201, 216-17

MacKinnon, Donald, 5-6, 92-93

Major subjects, 50-51

Marriage, 29-30, 43-44, 65, 197, 207, 234-35; age at, 58-59, 179-81; effect of, 183-88; see also Children; Family, marital; Wives

Medicine (respondents), 128, 129, 139

Military service, 23, 33, 55-56, 63, 65, 156, 208, 209, 212, 233-34; and GI benefits, 33, 42, 222; and doctorate, 54-56; respondents' reaction, 57-58; and career pattern, 82; and achievement level, 104-6, 207

Mobility, job, 213-14, 229-30, 237-38; and career pattern, 85-86; and achievement level, 109-10, 207; and future, 167-70; and career alternatives, 170-72

Motivation, 203, 217; see also Values

Music, 192, 193; see also Activities

Music (respondents), 40, 62, 73-74, 160, 171; see also Arts, the

National Science Foundation, 4-5

Native born, 34, 35, 99

Nature of work, 139, 141, 144-53, 159-60

Needs, vs. goals, 113-14, 173-74; see also Goals

Negroes, 45, 235-36

Newcomer, Mabel, 4

Nonprofit organizations (setting), 28, 93, 94-95, 149, 227

Nonwork activities, 132, 189, 190-94; see also Activities

Occupational Choice, 6-7, 22, 48, 49, 138

Occupational choice, 47-51, 203, 211-12; influences on, 37-39, 49, 52-54, 56-58; and age, 51-52, 80; and career pattern, 67, 80, 81-82, 83; changes of, 170-71; and achievement level, 203, 205
Occupational status of group, 27
Occupation of father, 35, 36, 37-39, 40-41, 99, 100-1, 207

Parent, death of, 35, 39-40, 41
Part-time work, 42-43
Patterns, 68-69; see also Career patterns
Performance, 7-8, 201-5, 210; potential, 10, 206, 210, 218
Personality, 103, 111, 218
Philosophy (respondents), 57, 126-27; family background, 38, 40; and work satisfactions, 139, 141, 143-44, 159
Physical sciences, 27; see also Pure sciences
Place of birth, 34-36, 38, 99
Policies, public, 233-37
Political activities, 191; see also Activities
Potential (performance), 10, 206, 210, 218
Poverty, 39, 236
Professional societies, 190; see also Activities
Professions, 27, 36, 99, 107, 108, 147, 148
Progression, in career, 67-69, 71, 168-70
Pure sciences, 83, 91, 107, 147, 237
Pure sciences (respondents), 53, 193; reaction to questionnaire, 18, 21; early education, 31, 32; family background, 35, 37, 38, 39, 41, 184; and career changes, 74-75, 77-78, 171; and achievement level, 94-95; and value orientation, 122-23, 128-29; and work satisfactions, 139-44, 159-62, 167; retirement and future, 169, 195

Quality of employing institution, 92, 93, 94-95

Quality of undergraduate college, 101
Questionnaire, 15, 19-20, 21-22, 23; attitudes of respondents toward, 18-19, 20-22, 23-24; reproduced, 241-50

Rank: military, 33, 105-6, 207, 213; occupational, 92, 169-70
Recreation, 189, 190-91; see also Activities
Religious activities, 189, 191; see also Activities
Religious affiliation of respondents, 45, 100
Research (function), 27, 84, 108-9, 115, 146-47
Research (respondents), 32, 53, 168, 185-86, 193; reaction to questionnaire, 18, 21; family background, 35, 39; and work satisfactions, 139, 141
Research and administration (function), 27, 85, 108-9, 147
Response mechanisms, 210-16
Responsibility, and achievement, 92, 93-95
Retirement, 177, 194-96, 198-99; see also Future
Rewards, 140, 142-52, 160-64, 173
Roe, Anne, 5

Salary (first job), 60-61; see also Income
Scholarships, 33, 102
Self-employed (setting), 28, 84-85, 87, 91, 93-94, 109, 149
Self-expression, 139, 141-42, 145-53, 173
Setting, institutional, 27-28, 84-85, 91-92, 93-94, 109, 149, 152
Shift, in career, 66-67, 172-73; examples of, 77-79; see also Career patterns; Mobility; Variant career pattern
Single men, 179, 180, 181
Social activities, 189, 191; see also Activities
Social contribution, 140, 142, 145, 147-52

Social reality, 206-10
Social sciences, 27, 91, 107, 147, 223, 237
Social scientists (respondents), 31, 53, 61-62, 185, 196; reaction to questionnaire, 18, 21; family background, 35, 38-39, 41-42, 44, 62; and military service, 42, 57-58; and work satisfactions, 139, 140-43, 159-62; and future, 169, 195
Social type, 119-20, 124-26, 130, 133-36, 152, 165, 180, 182, 188, 213
Sports, 189, 191-92, 193
Staff (function), 27, 108-9, 146, 148-49
Stance, 211, 212-14, 215-16
Status, 140, 143, 145-53, 160-63, 164-66, 169-70; see also Rank, occupational
Straight career pattern, 69-70, 71-72, 73-74, 80-86, 110-11, 134-35, 150, 163, 179, 186, 213
Superiors, relation to, 209, 229, 231

Talent, 1-2, 202; and genius, 219-21
Teachers, influence of, 52-53, 65
Teaching (function), 27, 84, 107-8, 110, 148
Teaching and research (function), 27, 84, 107-8, 110, 111, 149
Technical colleges, 31, 101, 111
Tenure, 231
Terman, L. M., 5
Time, role of, 47; military service, 33, 47, 104-5, 208, 209; acquisition of doctorate, 54-55, 65, 224; work dissatisfactions, 164-65
Time perspective, 211-12, 214-15

Tuition, 32-33, 223

Undergraduate preparation, 30-33, 50-51, 101
Upper achievement level, 93-111, 135, 151, 164-65, 180, 181, 187, 211-12, 213, 214

Value orientations, 9, 116-17, 132-36; and work satisfactions, 151-52, 164-65; and future, 157, 196; and marriage and children, 180, 182-83, 188; see also Ideological type; Individualistic type; Leadership type; Social type
Values, 112-15, 203; conflict in, 116-17, 128-29
Variant career pattern, 70-72, 76-87, 110-11, 134-35, 193, 195; and work satisfactions, 150, 163; marriage, 179, 181, 186-87; response mechanisms, 212, 213

War, effect of, 33-34, 56-58, 63
Warner, W. Lloyd, 4
War work, civilian, 33, 56
Wives who worked, 43-44, 58, 62, 181, 184
Work dissatisfactions, 140, 145, 162, 163, 165; intrinsic, 141-42, 146, 151, 160; extrinsic, 142-44, 145-46, 161-62, 164-65
Work-related activities, 189-90; see also Activities
Work satisfactions, 115, 137-39, 144-45, 147-53, 157; intrinsic, 139-40, 146, 149, 151, 153, 159-60, 163; extrinsic, 140, 146, 149, 151-52, 160-61, 163-65
World War II, 33-34, 62, 156